MOUNTAINS OF DAWN

MOUNTAINS OF DAWN

A PORTRAIT OF ARUNACHAL PRADESH

MAMANG DAI

SPEAKING TIGER

SPEAKING TIGER BOOKS LLP
125-A, Ground Floor, Shahpur Jat
New Delhi – 110049, India

This edition first published by Speaking Tiger Books, 2023

ISBN: 978-93-5447-652-5

10 9 8 7 6 5 4 3 2 1

Book and cover design and layout by Devashish Verma
Printed at Printworks New Delhi

This book is dedicated to the memory of my parents,
Odi and Matin Dai,
and to Arunachal Pradesh—
the land and its people.

CONTENTS

PREFACE TO THE NEW EDITION, 2023

I'll take all the time I please this afternoon
Before leaving my place alongside the river.
It pleases me, loving rivers.
Loving them all the way back
To their source.
Loving everything that increases me.'
—'Where Water Comes Together with Other Water', Raymond Carver

This book is being republished after almost a decade and a half. During this time Arunachal Pradesh has undergone tremendous change. It is a change that is both visible—with modern and technical assets—and diffuse, changing the lives of people in different ways, both obvious and subtle.

Ultimately, like all change, this one too is about movement and time. The new additions to the book are primarily about this, most recent, phase in the story of Arunachal.

PREFACE, 2009

Once known as the North East Frontier Agency (NEFA), Arunachal Pradesh became the twenty-fourth state of the country in 1987. In the early years of its history, the pace of change in the state was slow, somewhat cautious. We did not suffer displacement. The land was our birthplace. We worked the land and where we were was our home.

Today change has come like a steam roller. The transition from unknown frontier to modern state has been sharp and rapid and the question of direction and destiny has become one of great complexity and soul searching. On the one hand, in keeping with the national agenda, the state is forging ahead with goals for progress and development. On the other, the history of our people, our origins and routes of migration remain a matter of speculation, based purely on the few recorded documents left by early explorers. There are also specialized niches in our tribal heritage that may be erased forever if change is not assessed and negotiated carefully. This is the backdrop against which the modern history of the state is being written. And the question, always, is: 'Where do we begin, and what is the most important thing to start with?'

It is true that due to geographical and historical reasons the region has succeeded in keeping itself as one of the last bastions of the tribal world. But tribal society in the deep interiors is not entirely the serene, romantic picture that we might like to imagine. Life is very hard. Though the state also still enjoys the distinction of being one of the greenest parts of the country, the mountains offer little food. The isolation is like living in perpetual half light, prey to the elements and the unpredictable fury of nature. Yet, with faith and patience, a way of life was established that enabled the different communities to survive in a harsh terrain for centuries, with very little contact with the outside world.

This book is an attempt to record that way of life, which I perceive as a miracle of faith. This was not a faith that appeared like a bolt of lightning or as sudden enlightenment, or through the letters of an inherited text. It was a faith arrived at through a process of trial and error spanning centuries. I have drawn on oral narratives to illustrate this substance of faith; I have drawn on the art of the storyteller, the medicine man, the priest, where stories are linked to ritual and vice versa.

The book is draws upon my travel notes. Also included are accounts of some of the first explorers who stepped into this remote frontier and provided the first glimpses of this hidden land. But my true inspiration and guiding spirit are the words of Arunachal's villagers, who revealed to me that beyond the image of a rugged landscape and the aura of tribal life there is a highly ordered and organized system of functioning in the villages, a serene and solemn reconciliation with the environment and a deeply ingrained respect for human values evident in all tribal systems.

This book offers but a small glimpse of this life-world, but one that I hope will open a link with the reader. However hard one may try, any attempted portrayal can never be the complete picture. Nor can it be over, or finished. These words and stories are presented here as markers that a reader might draw on and expand, and perhaps rediscover an often mysterious landscape and imbue it with new insight and meaning.

PROLOGUE

THE STORY OF THE BEGINNING OF THE WORLD

The earth and the sky are husband and wife.

Formerly, Sedi, the earth, and Melo, the sky, lay close together and from their union every kind of tree and grass and living creature came into being. But so close was their union that there was no room for humankind to live. Then Polung Sabbo was born and wandered over the hills. His horns hit the clouds and in his anger he tossed them away, far above the earth. After being thus separated from her husband the sky, Sedi desired to return to him, to be one with him again, but as she was raising herself towards him the sun and moon appeared, and she was ashamed and could go no further. That part of her which was reaching towards her lord became fixed forever as the great mountains.[1]

I.

A HIDDEN LAND

The Mountain Dwellers

From where the mountains rise from the plains of Assam, stretching northward to the boundaries with China, lies India's furthest north-eastern state, Arunachal Pradesh.

It is a vast land. A land of austere grandeur and loveliness, covering 83,743 square kilometres that straddle the eastern Himalaya like a belt of green shadowed in perpetual rain and mist.

Village headmen of the early NEFA days; 1950s.

From its meeting point with Bhutan in the west, the state stretches 1,030 km eastward, descending from the northern boundary into the thickly forested slopes of the Patkoi hills, forming a triangular border with Bhutan, China and Myanmar. The area's remote geographical location, its inhospitable terrain, and the reported ferocity of its people left it outside the sphere of early exploration and evoked very mixed reactions from those who first gazed on this wild confusion of hills. It was 'the land of unknown savages, rugged, grand but uncultured', inhabited by 'strange shy creatures' who were 'very averse to receiving strangers'.[1]

The veil began to lift in the early part of the nineteenth century when interest in the region started with the exploration of the great river systems of the subcontinent and growing curiosity about the source of the river Brahmaputra. At the same time the first Anglo-Burmese war of 1824 opened up the entire north-eastern region of India for the first time. Agents of the East

Monpa boy with a pony.

India Company along with surveyors and cartographers began to push forward to explore this territory where no outsider had set foot before. The commercial success of tea cultivation in Assam furthered this interest. It was now felt that the tribes inhabiting the hill tracts were showing themselves to be dangerous neighbours whose marauding forays into the plains endangered the plans of the government to turn the rich Brahmaputra river valley into an immeasurable garden of silk and fragrant tea. The first recorded encounters between the hill people and outsiders date from around this time.

Jawaharlal Nehru in Ziro, sometime in the 1950s.

However, despite these early attempts to penetrate into the hills, the British Policy of Non-Intervention and the Inner Line Regulation Act of 1873 excluded the hill areas from proper administrative jurisdiction. The land continued to guard its mysteries well up to the time of India's independence. In terms of its unique cultural variety, scenic beauty and unexplored ecological wealth, Arunachal Pradesh remains, till today, a last great frontier of traditional culture.

Once known as the North East Frontier Agency (NEFA), Arunachal Pradesh became a union territory in 1972 and a full-fledged state in 1987. Arunachal Pradesh is the largest among what is grouped as the seven North-Eastern states or 'the seven sisters'. It is four times the size of Manipur, Mizoram, Meghalaya, and 500 sq km larger than the state of Assam. It is twice as big as Switzerland, Belgium or Denmark. It is home to twenty-six tribes spread across 5,589 villages, most of which are located in remote valleys and hilltops along the international borders with China, Myanmar and Bhutan.

The state is divided into sixteen administrative districts; moving west to east, these are: Tawang, West and East Kameng, Papum Pare, Kurung Kumey, Lower and Upper Subansiri, West, East and Upper Siang, lower Dibang Valley, Dibang Valley, Lohit, Anjaw, Changlang and Tirap. For practical purposes the area may be divided into three distinct cultural and artistic zones:

Sela Lake, Tawang.

Image of the Buddha in the Tawang Monastery.

THE WESTERN AND NORTHERN BOUNDARIES of high jagged peaks and lakes of ice. Here, in the districts of Tawang and West Kameng, the *Monpa* and *Sherdukpen* tribes are predominantly Buddhists of the Mahayana sect. West Kameng is also the home of the *Bugun (Khowa), Miji-Sajalong* and the *Hrusso (Aka)* tribes. 'Aka' means 'painted' and this was the name given by outsiders to the Hrusso because of their distinctive tattoo marks. Further north, in the district of Tawang, the famous Tawang monastery established in the seventeenth century is the largest in the country, controlling several gompas (monasteries) in the region. It is said that Mera Lama, the founder of the Tawang monastery, had a sister who became a nun. Any girl desiring to become a nun may enter the nunnery as a novice and there are three well known nunneries, or Am gompas in the Tawang area—Brama Dung Chung, Gyangong and Singsur Ani gompa.

Mountain flowers in Athu Popu, Dibang Valley.

EASTERN ARUNACHAL PRADESH in the uplands of the Patkoi mountain range bordering Myanmar and Nagaland. This part of Arunachal is lush with rainforest and is the land of the *Node, Wancho, Tangsa, Tutsa* and *Lisu (Yaobin*) tribes in the districts of Tirap and Changlang. The Tangsa have several sub tribes, like the *Muglom, Longchang, Mossang, Longphi, Kimchin, Tikhak, Ponthai, Lungri* and *Sangbal*. The famous biosphere reserve of Namdapha is located here and through this part of eastern Arunachal runs a portion of the famous Stilwell Road built by the Allies during World War II, linking Ledo in Assam to Kunming in the Yunnan province of China.

In this belt the south bank districts of Lohit, Lower Dibang Valley, Dibang valley and Anjaw on the Sino-Himalayan border are renowned for their spectacular scenery. Home to the *Idu, Taraon* and *Miju Mishmis;* the *Khamptis* and *Singphos;* and the *Meyors* who inhabit a few remote villages along the international border, this area was highlighted when a village hitherto unknown to the outside world, the village of Dong in Anjaw district, was identified as the country's sunrise village, receiving the first rays of the sun in the new millennium.

THE CENTRAL BELT spread over an extensive area covering the districts of East Kameng, Lower and Upper Subansiri, Papum Pare, Kurung Kumey, and East, West and Upper Siang. The major tribes living here are the *Nyishi, Tagin, Puroik, Hill Miri, Apa Tani, Nab (Nab Tagin),* the *Galo* and *Adi* tribes of *Bori, Bokar, Khamba, Memba, Padam, Pasi, Minyong Ramo, Pailibo, Shimong, Komkar, Milang, Panggi,* all of whom, except for the Memba and Khamba in Upper and West Siang districts, practise varying traditions yet are culturally akin due to the similarity of environment and the animistic nature of worship—they follow the belief of *Donyi-Polo,* the sun and moon. Known collectively as the *Tani* group, the tribes living here claim common ancestry from a legendary forefather known as *Abo Tani*, the first human being on earth.

Tsitapuri Lake, Upper Siang District.

Tribesmen of the frontier days.

The Origin of Tribes

The origin of the tribes of Arunachal is still shrouded in mystery. There are no conclusive records or research findings about their early history and progress of migration. It is, however, believed that they came from the triangle of Burma, where numerous Mongoloid tribal groups of similar culture lived in a widely dispersed area between the Salween, Mekong and Yangtze rivers.

The tribes may have dispersed due to population pressure, inter-tribal feuds and natural calamities. In the course of migration in search of better land, constant fighting, mutual fear and feuds among rival groups reduced their numbers and further separated them from one another. Most of the migratory routes of the tribes are largely traced through the oral literature of each tribe, though very often the names of places recorded in memory in the form of legends cannot be identified with anything recorded in modern maps.

In the Anini region of Dibang Valley, the Idu believe they had their origin in a place called *Inni-la-pon* to the north. In the course of their southward migration, they settled for some time at a place called *Kabbui-bui-Anda,* which means 'a place where the river flows backwards'. Perhaps this is a reference to a great bend in the river as it flows southwards from the Tibetan highlands. The Idu people also named the place *Jahiwi,* which means 'a place where the water snakes live'.

In Lohit district, the Khamptis claim Shan descent from the *Bor-Khampti* or 'Great Khampti', following a migratory route from a high valley in the mountains between the eastern extremity of Assam and the sources of the Irrawaddy river. The name Khampti is a composite of two words: *kham*—to stick; adhere to—and *ti*—spot; place. In another interpretation, Khampti means 'golden locality' *(kham*—gold—and *ti*—place).

Traditional masks of some tribes of Arunachal.

Legend has it that a tree of iron which yielded golden fruit grew in their country.
Their enemies, fearing that the Bor-Khamptis would become inordinately rich by means of this tree, sent a demon to devour them. The demon took up his abode in the gold-yielding tree and as he threatened to annihilate them, they were compelled, in self defence, to fell the tree in order to kill him. Legend says that the tree was felled by fire and the demon was then destroyed.[2]

Another story tells about an enormous bird that used to haunt the Bor-Khampti country, preying on children. This bird grew so rapacious that at last the whole country took up arms against it; but the bird was too clever and whenever it seized a child, it now began to fly off to a high hill called *Noi-Kham* (the golden hill) in the *Nam Yun* valley, on which grew an enormous tree whose branches were of silver and gold and which was held sacred by the Khamptis.

The bird would perch on the topmost branches of this tree, where it would devour its prey in safety. No other trees in the country were strong enough to bear the weight of this bird. So a general consultation was held and it was decided to sacrifice the sacred golden tree and cut it down so that the bird would leave the country or perch on some stone or rock where it would be easier to destroy.

So the tree was cut down. The bird tried in vain to perch on the branches of other trees, but they gave way under its weight. At last, in desperation, it perched on a huge slab of rock at the mouth of the Sada stream where it was killed. It is said the imprint of a child's foot and a bird's claw can be seen on a large rock at the mouth of the Nam Yun. The tree of gold disappeared but a small lake formed around it, overgrown with weeds, which in the cold season, when the water dries up, annually catches fire by spontaneous combustion.[3]

Among the Adis it is presumed that their original home was somewhere in Tibet. In their narrations the village elders often speak of the *Taro Mimats*, which is the name for the Tibetans, whose chief was known as Deba Lama. Although the Adi group trace their origin to Tibet, it is not clear what events compelled them to leave their original home. Some scholars have pointed to important events in Tibetan history in the seventh century AD that might have proved to be the turning point for many of the tribes that live in Arunachal Pradesh today. During this period Tibetan power was consolidated under the Yarlung dynasty and Buddhism was introduced as the state religion. These two events caused uprisings in central Tibet. The territory of Myang or Nyang was conquered by King Shrong-Tsan Gampo and annexed to the kingdom of Yarlung.

Adi hunters.

The Adis mention a land of *Misum-Miyang,* which, considering its geographical proximity, may be the Myang territory. The annexation of Myang and the conversion to Buddhism might have provoked the migration of groups of tribes who were caught in the struggle between Buddhism and the old shamanistic faith of Bonpo. Out of compulsion some stayed back and became Buddhists while others left, heading south group by group and at different times, sheltering in big caves and wandering like nomads before fanning out in different directions through the valleys of the Siang and Siyom rivers. Even today it is believed that there are Adi villages across the McMahon Line where they speak the same language and observe the same festivals.[4]

In February 2000, tribes and clans across the state came together to attend meetings called to discuss names and recognition for their various tribal identities. This activity was in preparation for a final list of tribes to be submitted to the Ministry of Tribal Affairs and subsequently became an Act of Amendment in the Parliament regarding the modification of tribes' names.

An Apa Tani priest (Nyibu) in traditional attire.

Children of the Galo tribe.

In the first Constitutional notification, 1950, only 12 Arunachal tribes were listed, these being the *Abor*, Aka, *Dafla*, Apa Tani, *Galong*, Monpa, Khampti, Singpho, Khowa, Sherdukpen, Mishmi and 'any Naga tribes'. On 21 November 1989, a second notification with certain modifications was proposed by the state government, which listed 25 major tribes and the name Adi instead of Abor. The Dafla and Galong of the first notification have also been replaced, in present usage, by the names Nyishi and Galo, respectively.

The first systematic census operation in Arunachal Pradesh started from 1961 onwards, though census operations were held in negligible pockets of the North-East Frontier Tracts under the Assam government. At that time, only tribes like Khampti, Miri, Naga, Pasi, Dafla, Mishmi and Singpho were enumerated in the Frontier Tracts of Sadiya and Balipara, and the old Lakhimpur, Darrang and Sibsagar districts.[5]

A Singpho woman with her dazzling mantle of silver ornaments (soi plong).

The first census reports of 1961 recorded a population of 3,36,558. The census in 2001 put the population of Arunachal Pradesh at 10,96,702, registering an increase by 3.26 times over 40 years. In the census of 2011, the state's population was 13,83,727.

Apa Tani woman with nose plugs made of bamboo root.

2.

THE CRADLE OF EVOLUTION

Sky Touching Trees

Nature has been bountiful to Arunachal Pradesh. The Himalayan region receives some of the world's heaviest rainfall and the result is an expanse of lush tropical forest where life breeds in myriad forms. The tangle of root, vine and decaying vegetation provides distinct ecological niches where life sustains itself in a delicate balance that is vulnerable to extinction by even the smallest threat to the habitat.

The endangered Bugun liochicla.

Leaf frog.

Lady's slipper orchid.

The state's unique position in a tri-junction endows it with overlapping Palaearctic, Indo-Chinese and Indo-Malayan features, making it the richest bio-geographical province of the Himalayan zone. With more than 400 species per 100 sq yards, it is comparable to any other rich biodiversity site in the world in richness of species. The state is identified as one of the two key bio-geographical zones within India rated among the world's top 18 biodiversity 'hotspots'. It is estimated that Arunachal harbours a minimum of 5,500 flowering species. It is a sanctuary of primitive flowering plants and a reservoir of wild genetic resources, many of which have not been catalogued yet.

Male Azure Sapphire.

An equally rich avifauna includes the country's highest number of pheasants, tragopans, monals, Bengal florican and the rare and endangered white-winged wood duck (in Namdapha). The picturesque Sangti Valley near Dirang in the West Kameng district is one of the six known wintering grounds of the black-necked Crane *(Grus nigricollis)*. The late Salim Ali had recorded over 500 bird species from the region. The state also abounds in a variety of reptiles, amphibians, butterflies, moths and beetles, aquatic and insect life.

The Great Indian Hornbill, the state bird of Arunachal Pradesh.

The forests of Arunachal are spread over 8.4 million hectares, covering a vast altitudinal variation from tropical and semi-evergreen forests to the greater Himalayan region of temperate vegetation to areas under permanent snow cover. Two species of pine—*Pinus merkusi* and *Abies delavavi*—are not found anywhere else in India.

The state also has some of the finest tropical evergreen forests in the low-latitude south bank tropical forests of the Tirap and Changlang districts and parts of the Lohit district. Here, specimens of Hollong *(Dipterocarpus macrocarpus*) grow to fabulous heights of over 60 metres with a girth of 9 metres. These are the 'sky-touching trees' whose silver-grey bole opens out into an oval crown that bears large fruit equipped with 'wings' that send seed spiralling downwards for future regeneration. The Hollong is an important commercial timber species. This mighty tree rears up above the forest, cutting off light for lesser trees like a 'selfish giant', but it is also the home of the Namdapha flying squirrel and its high canopy provides protective cover for the rare and shy Hoolock gibbon, the only ape found in Asia.

An Adi elder wearing a headdress of hornbill beak, boar tushes and goat hair.

The tribes of Arunachal Pradesh have always lived off the forest without posing any threat to the ecosystem. The tenets of traditional practice are deep-rooted in environment ethics supporting a close and harmonious relationship with nature. So far, the state's isolation has been the chief preserver of its magnificent environment. Arunachal still maintains a low population density of 17 per sq km (according to the 2011 census). A visitor here can still travel for many days without meeting a single person.

Landscape of Anjaw District.

However, with the increase in demand for timber and plant resources, natural threshold limits of forest systems are being crossed. The commercial extraction of timber has led to a marked reduction in forest area, raising urgent environmental concerns. Once, to cut down a big tree was taboo. Or it would be done after serious consultation amongst village elders and with the performance of prescribed rituals. Today, however, change has overtaken the state in a major way. In the heyday of timber operations a single Hollong tree fetched a price of Rs 65,000. In this lucrative business, vast tracts of forest have been destroyed forever. Development, road building and the influx of migrant labour have also contributed to habitat fragmentation, which has resulted in the disruption of stable biotic communities. One of the major casualties of deforestation is the loss of several endemic and economically important medicinal plants and herbs. Arunachal's tribes have a tremendous knowledge of the use of plants for native medicine. A large number of these plants are entered in the Red Data Book (a public document that is created for recording endangered and rare species of flora and fauna).

Bamboo grove, Ziro.

A premier institute of the state, the State Forest Research Institute (SFRI), has been making pioneering efforts in the field of survey and documentation of the state's biodiversity. At the same time, the institute is working in collaboration with WWF-India (Arunachal office), to provide locals with schemes that are income generating and sustainable alternatives to the use of forest products. Arunachal is known for naturally occurring orchids with over 525 species. The Orchid Research and Development Centre (ORDC) has piloted a number of projects on the feasibility of developing orchid farming as a commercial venture. An Orchid Research Centre set up in Tipi in the West Kameng district is the largest orchidarium in Asia. The institute has also been working on the genetic improvement of commercially important species of bamboo. Bamboo is used as food, fodder, fuel, and for fencing, and serves almost every requirement of the tribes, including construction. Of the 115 species of bamboo reported in India, 45 species in the wild are represented in Arunachal Pradesh, the highest among all the states of the country.

A north-east unit of the G.B. Pant Institute of Himalayan Environment and Development was also set up in the state in 1997. In addition to research activities and management strategies for natural resources in the Himalayan region, the institute also focuses on documentation of indigenous knowledge systems governing traditional resource use by local communities.

Tree Spirits

Evergreen forest in Pakke-Kesang district.

A belief prevalent among the tribes of Arunachal is that big trees are the dwelling place of spirits *(uyus, epom, yapom*). There are recurring stories of children being carried away by these spirits. In the village of Adi Pasi in the Upper Siang district, a number of such cases are spoken about. At such times, search parties are sent out to make a big noise, shouting threats and axing big trees. Sometimes the sacrificial rite of killing a pig or fowl is performed. If there is no deliverance, more trees are marked by sword blows. It is believed that such noise and vigour disturbs the tree spirits and provokes dissension amongst them, with the tree spirits of a particular area of forest arguing for the release of the human hostage so that the spirits are not displaced by the destruction of their habitat.

It is reported that some missing children return after an absence of three or four days. Inevitably, they come back in a trance-like state with no recollection of anything except that of a sound like wind rushing into the ears and a sensation of indescribable motion and freedom in the air. Older people who have been taken by the spirits and released also behave as if their wits had been stolen. Villagers, however, say that an indescribable odour clings to them and that such persons sometimes return carrying leaves of the *taan* tree or *ekkam,* which bodes well, for such a person will become wealthy and enjoy widespread fame. If a person is not so fortunate, he returns carrying twigs and wilting fern.

High Priority Biodiversity Areas

TALLEY VALLEY, LOWER SUBANSIRI DISTRICT

The Apa Tanis believe that the whole of the Apa Tani plateau was once under a huge lake. This lake was inhabited by a strange crocodile-like creature called the *Buru,* who burrowed underwater tunnels through the swamps and caused the hummocky appearance of the Apa Tani plateau. The first view of Talley valley gives the impression of a submerged land that has dried out over the years. Here, the altitudinal succession of vegetation is reversed; in an ecological phenomenon, the coniferous elements grow in the valley proper while the broad-leaved trees are seen above them on the hills and slopes, as if the hills had once sunk along with the vegetation.

Talley Valley (370 sq km) lies between the Subansiri, Sapu and Pange rivers, 30 km east of the district headquarters, Ziro. The valley is encircled by thickly wooded sloping hills and supports a distinctive valley swamp community. Following efforts undertaken by the Eastern Himalayan Programme of WWF-India and SFRI, this unusual area has been declared a wildlife sanctuary.

The first baseline survey reported a vast collection of species of shrubs, herbs and climbers, including 17 species of endangered plants and 21 species of wild relatives of crop plants. A species of bamboo (*Pleoblastus simonii)* is reported only from this valley in India. A rare rhododendron *(R. dalhousie)* also occurs only in the Talley valley.

The highlights of an avifauna survey were the first sighting in the state of the purple cochoa *(Cochoa purpurea)* and record of the second location of the yellow rumped honey guide *(Indicator xanthonotus)*. A number of other rare birds breed here, and this has added to the significance of the Talley valley as a breeding habitat.

Yellow-rumped honey guide.

DI CHU VALLEY, ANJAW DISTRICT

The Di Chu Reserve takes its name from the Di Chu stream that originates in Myanmar and flows westwards to join the Negi Chu river flowing from China. The valley is contiguous with the forests of the Kachin state of Myanmar, and the Yunnan province of China. Di Chu marks the boundary between the no-man's land bordering China and India before merging into the Lohit river, which cuts through the district of the same name. This tri-junction region is unusually rich in medicinal plants, specifically along a 30-mile stretch from the settlements of Melinja to a place called Hotspring. Ginseng *(Panax sikkimensis* and *P. pseudoginseng),* Mishmi teeta (*Coptis Teeta*), Aconite *(Aconitum napellus Linn)*, Berberis and *Taxus baccata,* are all found here within an altitudinal variation of 2,100 metres to 3,100 metres.

The Mishmi takin.

This valley is also the habitat of all the three goat antelopes found in India: the Mishmi Takin *(Budorcas taxicolor),* the Serow *(Capricornis sumatraensis)* and the Goral *(Nemorhaesus goral).* The Takin, a large bovid weighing up to 650 kg and found in the Mishmi hills is a relative of the musk ox, and some naturalists believe that: the Takin's golden coat might be the golden fleece of Greek mythology. A new bird record for India has also come from this area: the Elliot's laughing thrush *(Gerrulax ellioti),* which earlier had been reported only from across the border, in

Clouded leopard.

NAMDAPHA NATIONAL PARK, CHANGLANG DISTRICT

Namdapha takes its name from the Dapha Bum ridge at the tri-junction of the Irrawaddy, Brahmaputra and Lohit river basins. The park was created in 1983 as the fifteenth tiger reserve of the country. Declared a biosphere reserve, the park harbours a phenomenal range of biota from tropical wet evergreen forest to tablelands of glaciers and snow-covered peaks, the highest of which is 4,751 metres. The total park area is 1,985 sq km. Most of the species found here are rare, endangered or vulnerable. Hollong trees are also concentrated in this pocket of pristine forest south of the river Brahmaputra and are not found anywhere else. Survey results also suggest that Namdapha is the only park in the world that supports the four great felines within one reserve, viz., the tiger, leopard, clouded leopard, and snow leopard.

In addition to these reserves, Arunachal Pradesh has 11 wildlife sanctuaries and national parks, covering a total geographic area of approximately 8 per cent under the Protected Areas Network in India. Apart from these sanctuaries, the inaccessible and uninhabited parts of Arunachal—from high, icy grasslands to wetland sites—remain important wildlife habitats whose isolation so far serves as the best protection for the state's ecological wealth.

Noa Dihing river in Namdapha.

3.
MYTHS OF CREATION
In the Realm of the Gods

'There is a dreamtime,
A land of fish and stars—
It is from there
That we have come
To live on this earth.'
(Old Adi belief)

In the beginning, there was only Keyum, or nothingness. It was neither darkness nor light, nor had it any colour or movement. Keyum is the remote past beyond the reach of our senses. It is the place of ancient things from where no answer is received. Out of this great stillness the first flicker of thought began to shine like a light in the soul of man. This shimmering trail took shape and expanded to what is known as the pathway. Out of this nebulous area a spark was born that was the light of imagination. It grew into a shining stream that was the consciousness of man, and from this, all the stories of the world and all its creatures came into being.[1]

The shamans as storytellers.

The myth as primitive history expressed in poetic form is notable among the tribes of Arunachal Pradesh. Myths of the origin of the world, the sky, the heavenly bodies are recounted by professional rhapsodists on a variety of occasions, especially during the time of the great festivals. The notion of the earth emerging out of a primeval ocean or a macrocosmic world transformed by the sacrifice of some great personage is a common motif. A few stories speak of an original world destroyed by flood or fire, while a Singpho tale attributes the direct creation of the earth and sky to a universal mother who figures in other interpretations as the earth mother or the rain mother.

At first there was neither earth nor sky, only cloud and mist. From it a woman called Khupning-Knam was born in the form of a cloud. In time she gave birth to a girl and a boy who had the appearance of snow. When they grew up they married and from them were born a girl called Inga (earth) and a son called Mu (sky). Inga was mud, and Mu, a cloud. Together they had a boy called Imbung, the wind. When he was born he blew so strongly that he raised the cloud, his father, into the sky and dried up his mother, the mud. In this way heaven and earth were made.[2]

Among the Tani group of tribes, sub tribes and clans, a rich store of oral literature explains every natural phenomenon in a series of narrative songs and folktales. A story becomes a storehouse of many meanings, and the reasons for the rituals and ceremonies in the observance of traditional practice are contained in these stories. An example of this was revealed during one festival when I asked an old man why he was not eating with the others. He was sitting in the sun working on some bamboo.

'I cannot sit idle,' he said. 'I think I'll make a basket.'

'Would you like something to eat?'

'I would,' he said, laughing, 'but I am recovering from a dog bite and it is taboo for me to eat pork now.'

'But didn't you take injections?'

He said that he had, but there were other things to consider. He said he knew people who had taken injections but still died from rabies because they did not observe the taboos.

What taboos?

The old man's reply came in the form of a story about a dog and a pig.

Elderly man weaving a cane basket.

'You see, the dog and the pig are bitter enemies. A long time ago the pig would furrow the earth, dig and crumble the soil and prepare it for sowing. The dog lay about all day doing nothing. Who knows, he might even have taunted the poor pig as he sweated at his labours. Then, at the right moment, the dog leapt up and ran round the field yapping like a lunatic, leaving his footprints on the soft, moist earth. When man (tani) returned from hunting, he saw that the dog had been very active and hardworking and decided to reward him by inviting him into the house to share his fire. The poor pig, slandered as a good-for-nothing, was left outdoors to root around in aggrieved frustration. Such is the story. Our beliefs may seem simple but they are based on experience, and there are stories to prove it. It is important to keep the taboos. The two animals are bitter enemies and it's not good to mix up these things.'

Perhaps the old enmity, like poison, fights again in a man's body if he is reckless enough to eat the meat of a pig after being bitten by a rabid dog. If a man breaks the taboo and dies, then it is his punishment for that terrible error of judgement that his forefather made long ago, which is recorded only in these stories.

Today, temples and churches can be seen all around the state. Yet the ties with the past are not completely severed. In the towns and district headquarters, major festivals are celebrated on officially notified dates with cultural events performed for local and visiting dignitaries. The true meaning of the celebrations, however, may be found more in the remote villages, which generally are no more than a clearing in the forest or a few scattered houses perched on a hilltop. Here, surrounded by the dark forest with little or no communication even with the nearest village, life is still harsh and unpredictable. Man lives in the company of gods and spirits, both good and bad. In such surroundings, the rites of propitiation, knowing one's obligation and observing age-old taboos acquire great importance.

The songs and myths of our tribes illuminate and explain natural phenomena—why the mountains are high, why snakes bear an enmity to man, why men weep, why we die, why killing a tiger is equivalent to killing a man.

Everyone knows the stories, in one form or another, and this knowledge links the individual to a group. But most often the stories are so inseparable from the routine of daily life that they are not perceived as stories any more. Over a period of time, the myths evolved into a set of beliefs through which certain concepts became the basis for customary practice observed by the tribes. Without these articles of faith, life would be meaningless chaos.

Customary Laws

Apa Tani and Nyishi gaon buras in the late 1950s.

Although there are no fences visible, all of the territory of Arunachal Pradesh is invisibly marked. Every tribe knows its village boundaries, and whose land is where, be it individual or clan land. Similarly, the rivers are marked and every tribe and clan knows which land or stretch of the river is ancestral property, over which that particular clan alone has hunting and fishing rights.

Among the tribes of Arunachal Pradesh, a highly developed system of village councils functions as a guide to relations, kinship, moral standards, and regulation and integration of group activities. This is notable among the *Kebang* of the Adi, the *Buliang* of the Apa Tani, *Mele* of the Aka, *Yallo* of the Nyishi, *Phrai* and *Kabaya* of the Miju and Taraon Mishmi respectively, *Abbala* of the Idu, *Ngothun* of the Nocte, *Khapho, Khaphong, or Khaphongwa,* of the Tangsa, and *Ngajowa* of the Wanchos, amongst others.

Up until 1972, Arunachal Pradesh had no police force. The Councils were responsible for the maintenance of peace and harmony amongst members of society and were empowered to settle disputes of any sort with the help of their customary laws, which provide a system of administrative norms for 'laws of birth and disposal of the dead, marriage, property rights and inheritance, laws of settlement and rehabilitation, laws of criminal offence, laws of worship, freedom of expression and arbitration and laws of social service for the smooth management of society'.[3]

Each village has its own tribal council, which is essentially a Council of Elders functioning as a court of the people. Its members are the headmen appointed to represent every clan in the village. The members of a kebang cannot exercise powers to collect land revenue or house tax, but are empowered to impose fines and punish the guilty. The decision of the kebang is binding on every individual living within its jurisdiction. A group of villages comprises a *Bango,* and above this is the apex body of the *Bogum-Bokang,* which functions as a parliament attended by all the leading men representing every section, and dealing not only with inter-village disputes but also taking up important questions of development. Kebangs are traditionally held in the bachelors' dormitory known as *moshup,* which also functions as a community hall. Any aggrieved party is entitled to call a kebang. The speakers are chosen for their knowledge, honesty and experience, and their powers of oration.

'It is like a sugar press,' one elder explains. Every word is weighed, measured, refined. Every speaker is given his turn and he waves his arms, taps his foot and his oratory is rhythmic and skilled. Justice is the goal, and conviction and persuasion come from the power of words. Across the state these councils worked within the framework of the Assam Frontier (Administration of Justice Regulation Act), 1945. Under this Regulation it was laid down that: 'The proceedings of the village authority need not be recorded in writing.' A kebang was more than a mere discussion of evidence and guilt. It was, in fact, an exercise in logic, philosophy, democratic principles and intellectual curiosity whose proceedings could last for a day, weeks, even months.

Today, of course, modern law and the introduction of panchayati raj have led to inevitable changes in the social and political systems of the tribes. The performance of a village council, its rules and codes of conduct were derived from oral traditions which, in today's world, may be unable to deal with crimes that have no precedence in tribal society. However, traditional village councils are still functioning side by side with panchayat bodies within the same area and 'a plaintiff can still approach the traditional councils freely for quick settlement of disputes at village level or between clan members. The institution of Gaon Buras (village headmen), appointed for their calibre and influence in society is also still active and a number of women—'Gaon Buris'—have joined the ranks since the establishment of the Gaon Bura committee in 1980, to ensure greater involvement and equal representation of women in decision making bodies.

Bride Price

Apa Tani man with his wives.

Once upon a time the birth of a child was announced by symbols that were placed at the entrance of the house of the newborn. People passing the house would know if it was a male child by the symbol of a miniature bamboo bow and arrow. A small, woven rain hat announced the birth of a baby girl. This custom was called *tasar ragnam.* It is not observed now but the symbols retain their significance and can be interpreted as symbols of one's destiny. In traditional society a woman receives protection and shelter within the framework of traditional rules and practice. There is no dowry system among the Arunachal tribes. There is, however, a reverse of dowry in the marriage laws that requires the family of the prospective groom to pay bride price in the form of *mithun,* cloth, and valuable utensils. The social implication of bride price is that a daughter is considered an economic asset and by giving her away in marriage, her family must be compensated in kind. Sometimes situations crop up that create trouble. For instance, the practice of child marriage whereby consenting parents betroth their children to each other, sometimes even before birth; or a

Life in the mountains can be hard, and often the women bear the most burden.

young girl to a man more than twice her age. In many cases an unwilling bride might run away or ultimately elope with somebody else, in which case the aggrieved husband must be compensated by the return of the original bride price. Sometimes the groom's family is unable to pay the price negotiated for a daughter. In such cases the village councils are called upon to settle disputes and arrive at mutually acceptable agreements. In some extreme cases the husband would abduct the girl from her house or from the fields and keep an unwilling bride under captivity, which was called *tapya parnam/lapya tanam*. This was a form of punishment among some tribes where the left leg of the woman was tied or fitted into a heavy log that prevented her from walking without help from others. In such cases the girl's parents were unable to do anything. This punishment could continue until the girl was forced to agree to a marriage or the demands of the husband, and sometimes continued even after the birth of one or two children. Sometimes this forcible bondage resulted in the death of the woman.

Arunachal society is patriarchal and the descent is traced through the male line. The laws of inheritance are strict and in the event of a husband's death, a widow cannot inherit her husband's property though she can have usufructuary rights over the property while she is alive and is willing to stay in the same family, or until her sons have attained adulthood. In no case can a widow pass property on to her daughters. Only personal possessions, those that were given as marriage gifts in the form of ornaments, utensils and implements of weaving, etc., can be handed down to her daughters. In the absence of sons, only her husband's brothers or his nearest relatives can inherit property.

A Nyishi woman with her children.

In the event of adultery committed by a woman, she is deprived of the usufructuary right over property and also has to pay back all the bride price to her deceased husband's relatives. An additional fine may also be imposed on her. Usually the bride price and the fine imposed is paid by the new husband or her parents with whom she might intend to rehabilitate herself.

Sajalong (Miji) girls of West Kameng.

Today, Arunachal's women have come a long way from the days of forced marriage and bondage. A State Commission for Women was constituted in 2005, and with time the status and representation of women is changing, along with life style and attitudes. Given the opportunity, Arunachal women are inherently geared to multi-task. Many women have become the breadwinners of the family. And while life in the remote villages is still linked to the major activities of the agricultural cycle and much remains to be done in the field of education, legal aid, health and child care, many Arunachal women today are entering the modern labour market, engaging in trade and commerce, entrepreneurial business, and striking out for civil and political empowerment and a share in decision making.

The Laws of Burial

Death, in tribal society, is an event that is shared by all. Relatives pour into the house of the deceased and keep a 'wake' that can last for many days. The bereaved family prepares food and wine and fires are lit to accommodate guests all through the night. A special feature is the *penge* or songs of lamentation that are sung as impromptu verse by relatives or close friends of the deceased, recalling the days of childhood, remembering various incidents and the time that they spent together.

Apart from the Buddhist tribes there is no belief in reincarnation among the other tribes. The after-life is believed to be similar to life here on earth. There, a man will meet his ancestors and loved ones again after he passes through the narrow gate called *Sedi Litung Borbung* or *Yamo Limang Borkok* with the guidance of gods and goddesses. Among some tribes it is believed that tattoos are the only signs by which a person will be recognized by kith and kin in the after-life.

Nocte woman with facial tattoos (above) and man with an elaborate tattoo on his chest.

It is customary practice to bury the possessions of a dead man with his body. A small bamboo thatch shelter is erected over the grave and clothes, beads, hats, guns and spears, and other earthly belongings are hung over the tomb. Otherwise the spirit of the dead man may return to haunt his descendants since they did not equip him adequately to start life in the other world.

The noted anthropologist Dr Verrier Elwin narrates how he once saw a remarkable basket decorated with wooden skulls and bear's fur in a Wancho village. When he tried to buy it, offering a very high price, the owner, an old and poor man, refused to sell, saying that in a few months he would be dead and that unless the bag hung on his tomb he would be without credit in the other world.[4]

The Story of the Celestial Aunt[5]

At the dawn of human existence there sprang up on the surface of the earth an ancient human society known as the *Kojum-Koja.*

A priest leading a sacred dance.

The Kojum-Koja established villages and were a self-sufficient, contented and happy people. The Kojum-Koja civilization was destroyed by a devastating flood let loose by the ruler of the waters *Biri-Bote.* The only one to survive the destruction was a charming beauty known as *Nyangi Myete,* or the celestial aunt, who glided down to the human family of *Doni-Dongor.* Dressing herself in the fashion of a glamorous bride wearing a white silken skirt with a green border, and possessing all the qualities of civilized life, the celestial beauty floated down to bring grace and warmth to the society of humans. Indeed, her arrival generated a new current of life and enthusiasm among the people she visited.

THE GREAT FLOOD: An important part of the social life of the people of Kojum-Koja was the observance of festivals marked by community singing and dancing. One day, they laid fish traps in preparation for the *Pi-me* festival, and a huge, fish-like creature with a peculiar appearance was captured in one of the traps. It was taken to the village where it was identified as Biri Angur Potung, the son of the powerful ruler of the waters. He was killed and his flesh consumed during the festival.

At this time a guest appeared amongst the society of Kojum-Koja. It was the bat, Koru Ponsung Babu. The guest inquired about the meat and how they had enjoyed the festival. The people of Kojum-Koja replied that a fish had been caught in their traps and that they had killed it for the festival. After hearing this the guest left, as scheduled, for the domain of the water *(silli-sidong).* Arriving in the deepest depths, the bat noticed the wife of the ruler of the watery regime weeping in great sorrow. The queen was asking who had kidnapped her beloved son, Biri Angur Potung. The bat broke the news to her that her son had been killed and consumed in a festival by the Kojum-Koja.

The news of the killing of Biri Angur Potung sparked off a great war. News of the tragedy reached every nook and corner of the watery regime and its ruler commanded his war generals to launch a terrifying attack on the people of Kojum-Koja. With sharp, dazzling blades and rattling swords the combined armies unleashed their fury wave after wave on the land of Kojum-Koja. The Kojum-Koja defended themselves valiantly, but the armies of the great king besieged them from all sides. In the form of rain, storm, flood and erosion, the armies of the waters destroyed the land of the Kojum-Koja and buried their civilization.

Out of this wreckage a lady emerged like a lonely reed. She was the popular beauty known as Nyangi Myete, celestial bride of the Kojum family who drifted down to humanity to tell the tale of destruction, and to generate new hope for another civilization on earth. Tradition presents her as the most charming and beauteous bride of the Kojum-Koja. She is viewed as the centre of attraction and the warmth of the society revolves around her. It is Nyangi Myete who pleases guests and friends by pouring out cups of rice wine while her charismatic and entertaining manner maintains the honour and humour of the society. It is her generosity that makes people dance and sing and enjoy life. The land and people of Kojum-Koja may have been buried in the deluge, but because of this celestial lady, the memory of that civilized society remains immortal.

From the obscure world of myth, this celestial lady came down to live on this earth. Her beauty is present in the forms of natural things. The green vegetation on the surface of the earth is the green-bordered skirt that she wears. Her silken white robe is transformed into clouds. The changes of the seasons are her appearance on different social occasions. The water and rain are her sweat and tears. Her melodious songs and music are transformed into the sweet voices of birds and humming insects. The ever changing and beautiful natural world represents the Kojum-Koja. Thus, mythological belief is projected into lived reality through natural surroundings and human imagination.

Nyangi Mete, the Celestial Bride.

Sangestar Lake, on the way from Tawang to Bum La Pass.

4.

A FORBIDDING & FASCINATING WORLD

'...undoubtedly less corrupt than Paris'[1]

In 1853 Nicholas Michael Krick, a young Jesuit priest, made an observation in a publication that succinctly summed up the era of exploration and travel of the north-eastern region that began in the nineteenth century. He wrote: 'Since the English first occupied Assam twenty-nine years ago several agents of the East India Company have tried to gain access into this country with a view, if possible, to enter into commercial relations with *Thibet,* and to ascertain whether the *Siang,* known to the English by the name of *Dihong* is really the famous *Zang-po,* which crosses *Thibet* from east to west, and which has been such a puzzle to geographers of the last centuries.'[2]

An Adi man with a dao (sword) strap decorated with tiger teeth.

A Nyishi girl with bow and arrow.

Father Krick added that the tribes of the Siang area, specifically the Padam Abor (Adi) had astutely read the signs of the times, arguing that if they allowed any Englishman to penetrate into their country under any pretext, he was sure to have an army at his heels. 'In their opinion any white skin, any nose somewhat protruding, is of English make. This will make you understand the trouble I had in getting their consent to receive me. My cross, so similar to theirs, and my reputation of a French priest were my only passport.'

Krick was also trying to make his way to Tibet through the territory of the Mishmis, a neighbouring tribe of the Padam Abors. Born in 1819, in Lixheim, France, he became a member of the Societe des Missions Etrangeres, and had come to India in 1850 as Superior of the South Tibetan Mission. Travelling alone and on foot, carrying only his cross, a flute, sextant and medical chest, Krick succeeded in reaching the remote settlement of Oualong (Walong) on the northern Mishmi hills and almost reached Rima, a small Tibetan administrative centre. At this point, however, he seemed to have run out of his resources and was asked to leave the country. It was during his return to the plains that Krick paid a visit to Membu (Mebo), a village of the Padam Abors on the banks of the river Siang. Here, he was well received and during his short stay, he cured a number of sick people and made his famous notes on the tattoo marks worn by Padam men and women which he likened to the Maltese, Lorraine and St Andrews Cross. His account provides one of the first records of the Abors: 'the Padams are naturally hospitable; the guest is first expected to give a present to make friends with the host, but it is the meal that sanctions and seals friendship forever; as soon as you have touched food, "you are friends till the sun falls", as these savages are wont to say... They seem to possess much of the child's simplicity, and *Membu (Mebo)* is undoubtedly less corrupt than Paris.'

British troops with the first gun carried to the hills.

In January 1854 the intrepid Father set out again for Tibet, this time accompanied by Fr Augustin Bourry. A friendly Mishmi chief escorted them and they reached the Zayul valley. Unfortunately, this time, the two Fathers seem to have offended a powerful Mishmi chief whose name is spelt variously in the records as *Kaisa, Kahesha* and *Kai-ee-sha.* Through a misunderstanding, Kaisa felt that he had been double-crossed by the two men who had invited him to take them over the Tho-Chu pass, promising him money and guns. The angry chief followed the Fathers into Tibet and killed them as they were returning along the Tellu path by the mouth of the Tho-chu.

The following year, under instructions from Lord Dalhousie, a small party of the Assam Light Infantry, led by Lieutenant F.G. Eden set out from Sadiya to track down Kaisa. Kaisa was taken to Dibrugarh in Assam where he was tried for the murder of the Frenchmen and thrown into prison and sentenced to death. At the time, the Paris Foreign Mission had pleaded for the punishment to be commuted to life imprisonment but Kaisa was finally hanged for having murdered his jailer.

The story of Nicolas Krick and Augustin Bourry might have disappeared into history if not for a mysterious turn of events more than 143 years after their death in Mishmi territory. On 27 December 1997, a mass by a priest from the Paris Foreign Mission was conducted in a makeshift church of bamboo and tin-sheet roof in Tezu, Lohit District for the first Catholics of the Mishmi tribe. A few months later, fifteen baptisms were celebrated in the same chapel. Events had come full circle. Today Nicolas Krick and Augustin Bourry are regarded as the first martyrs of Arunachal Pradesh and the fathers of the faith in a land where they endured so much hardship and eventually lost their lives.[3]

The first recorded history of this frontier is thus linked with the feats and failures of the early days of exploration. All of the districts of Arunachal have their stories to tell about these first encounters. There were the good contacts and overtures of friendship, and there was fear and suspicion, and conflicts that ended in tragedy, reprisals and death. The lure of the place lay primarily in its isolation. It was *terra incognita.* The big rivers that cut through the Himalayan watershed and criss-cross the state also exercised a strange fascination that drew travellers to travel vast distances through unknown territory.

A Mishmi couple, sometime in the 1920s.

THE HEART OF WATER

In the heyday of geographical exploration, one of the mysteries that captured the imagination of cartographers and surveyors was the course of the river Tsangpo of Tibet. It was assumed that the Brahmaputra of Assam and the Tsangpo river were one and the same, and that the connecting channel between the two rivers was the river Siang of Arunachal covering some 300 miles of unexplored territory in the land of the Adis. No survey could be conducted along this stretch as every attempt made by the British to proceed up river from the plains of Assam was blocked by armed warriors and this unknown portion of the river became known, in the terms of the Survey of India, the 'missing link' guarding the mystery of the Tsangpo-Brahmaputra connection.

Cane bridge over the river Siang. Early visitors to the region remarked on these 'marvels of engineering'—suspension bridges made of thick strands of cane lashed with twine.

The Siang valley is the home of the Adi people, (formerly Abor), comprising the Minyong, Pasi, Padam, Karko, Shimong, Bori, Bokar, Ramo, Tangam, Pailibo, Panggi, Milang, Komkar tribes who are settled here in a number of villages on the banks of the Siang and its tributaries. Beyond the furthest village is the formidable mountain wall that forms India's boundary with China. Here the Tsangpo river cuts through the main Himalayan range in a deep and narrow gorge between the peaks of Gyala-Peri and Namche Barwa, turning into Indian territory at the town of Gelling in Upper Siang district, from which point it is called the Siang. In the Adi language, Si-Ang is interpreted as 'the heart of water'[4] or Taro Siang, 'the eternal river.'[5]

THE EXPEDITIONS

On 5 April 1827, a small expedition set out from the town of Sadiya in Assam on the banks of the river Brahmaputra. Sadiya was the first British post established in the region in 1822 to maintain relations with the hill tribes. The members of the expedition were Phillip Burlton, aged 21, Junior Lieutenant (Artillery), and Richard Wilcox, a young surveyor. Their mission was to travel through Mishmi territory in the hills north of Assam and cross the Patkoi mountain range into Burma to prove that the Irrawaddy river of Burma was unconnected with the Brahmaputra of Assam. Then the case for the Tsangpo-Siang-Brahmaputra connection would be that much stronger.

Dense tangle of tree, root and vine, of the kind that early expeditioners would have had to cut through.

The two men headed eastward, cutting their way through the dense undergrowth of wild cane. It was the onset of the monsoons and the two officers experienced all the hazards of journeying through tropical jungle during the rains. They suffered swollen feet, fevers, sores, and were tortured by the persistent clouds of gnats called *dim-dams* that left them no rest. An elephant they had arranged for to accompany them kept slipping on the steep, slippery slopes and, afraid that the animal might strangle itself with its load, they had to abandon it. Leeches clung to them. On one occasion, thirty-five of the bloodsuckers were torn from one leg. Wilcox became lame from dim-dam bites and Burlton suffered from fever. Nevertheless, the two men pressed on, followed the Irrawaddy to its source and proved conclusively that the river of Burma was unconnected with the river of Assam. Once back in Sadiya, they compiled their reports with Burlton closing his journal with a grim warning against attempting such a journey as the chances were 'very much against a man returning alive'.[6]

In 1911 another expedition marched into the hills cutting their way through the chaos of virgin forest along the banks of the river Siang in the territory of the Adis. They were the men of a punitive expedition called the Abor Expeditionary Field Force, sent to avenge the murder of Noel Williamson, Assistant Political Officer, whose survey mission into the hills had ended in tragedy in the village of Komsing.

Noel Williamson was the first British officer to reach this village. A member of the Indian Police Service, he was also a scientific cartographer and trained in the Government of India's Survey Department. In a long and distinguished career in the hill tracts, he had made many successful journeys, tracking the unexplored course of the Siang river and maintaining friendly relations with the tribesmen.

On this occasion, Williamson was accompanied by a colleague, Dr Gregorson, a tea garden doctor, and forty-seven sepoys and porters. Except three survivors, all of them were killed in an encounter with the tribesmen.

Today the cause for the attack is a matter of conjecture. The few available records point to a series of misunderstandings that provoked suspicion and anger among the tribesmen. When news of the massacre reached British authorities almost a month later, the Lieutenant Governor stationed at Shillong, Meghalaya, Sir Lancelot Hare, immediately consulted Major General Hamilton Bower, Commander of the Assam Brigade. On 24 July 1911, the Government of Eastern Bengal and Assam, supported in turn by the Government of India, approved and sanctioned the preparations for the expedition, which drew troops from the Naga and Gurkha Battalions of the Indian Army as well as a Company of King George's Sappers and Miners.[7]

The wife of an officer attached to the Abor expedition wrote: 'It is such a bore that my husband has to go off on that silly Abor Expedition to fight those stupid aborigines with their queer arboreal habits...'[8] At this time, royal greetings for Christmas from King George also arrived for the General Officer Commanding of the Abor expeditionary forces with the inclusion of a line, 'looking for a successful and speedy termination of the expedition'.

The news of the approaching troops spread like wildfire through all the villages in the area. The Adis were not slow to prepare for battle and they lined the jungle tracks with hundreds of fire-hardened bamboo stakes that could pierce through footwear and incapacitate the unfortunate victim. They cut bridges, blocked paths with heavy logs and placed poisoned arrows where they would fly at the enemy triggered by the slightest movement. They fortified their positions on high cliffs with enormous rock chutes that could set off an avalanche of boulders on the advancing columns below.

In the end, the unwavering troops of Major General Bower, and their inexorable advance wore down the resistance of the Adis. Slow and methodical, General Bower inspired his men to withstand the torment of leeches, mosquitoes and poisonous insects while hacking their way through the dense jungle with *daos* and shovels and, on occasion, dynamite, clearing 35 km in one month. By Christmas 1911 the Abor war was over and village chiefs surrendered, bearing flags of old newspapers.

On 10 January the following year, another column struggled up the steep path into Komsing village. They were a party of six British officers and six Signallers with 100 rifles of the 1st Battalion of the 8th Gurkhas, and 150 porters under the command of Lieutenant Colonel Murray. Colonel Murray carried with him a stone on which was carved:

'On this spot was murdered Noel Williamson
Assistant Political Officer, Sadiya,
March 31st, 1911'

It was an impressive ceremony. The headman and villagers were assembled before Colonel Murray and his officers. The buglers sounded the 'First Post', a general salute followed, and the troops presented arms. The memorial cairn was then unveiled and Colonel Murray addressed the headman, instructing him that the upkeep of the memorial was his responsibility. At the end of the address, the buglers sounded the 'Last Post', and the officers bared their heads. A similar cairn was unveiled where Dr Gregorson met his fate but river floods have since carried away all traces of the tragedy and the memorial to the intrepid doctor. The old post of Sadiya was also washed away by floodwaters during the great earthquake of 1950.

An interesting feature of the Abor expedition was the use of compressed tea. Since all supplies had to be portered through the most inhospitable terrain, tea consignments for the troops became the subject of unusual experiment. The firm of Lipton was given permission by the Government of India to provide supplies of compressed tea instead of loose leaf. A special machine was sent to India for the purpose of compressing the tea which could then be transported in chests of 45 pounds each, measuring a mere 20 inches by 15 inches by 8 and a half inches. It was the first time that troops on service in India were given compressed tea.

Peace envoy of the surrendering Adi villages in 1911.

With the surrender of the Adi villages along the Siang, the long-awaited exploration of the region began. Survey missions were dispatched into remote valleys and the unexplored river systems of Abor territory, and simultaneously into the Lohit and Subansiri districts. The prospect of solving the mysteries of the Tsangpo river became a reality and some 3,500 sq. miles of country was mapped on a scale of four miles to the inch. With further exploration upriver and from the Tibetan side in 1912-13, the last doubts about the exact course of the Tsangpo were effectively settled and the mystery of the Tsangpo-Brahmaputra connection brought to an end.

Today, the entrance to the Komsing village is alive with the sound of children marching to school. The giant bamboo field where the British forces camped before the final ascent to the village is green and tranquil. The memorial cairn to Noel Williamson remains where it had been placed, on a hill overlooking the longhouse where Williamson rested and the spot near where he was struck down.

The Power of Water

On 11 June 2000, the Siang river unleashed havoc in the area when flash floods hit the three districts of East, West and Upper Siang. The village of Komsing was totally cut off when the bridge linking it to the rest of the district was swept away. The country's longest cable steel suspension bridge spanning 207 metres and held up by twelve suspension cables 21 metres above high flood level was also torn apart and washed away. Within a period of nine hours, the water level rose by more than forty metres. According to eyewitness accounts, the fury of the floodwaters uprooted enormous trees and carried them, packed tightly together in a black, churning current that gave the impression of an entire forest sweeping down at great speed. The roar of the water could be heard in all the distant villages perched

By the same evening, the waters receded, but all eleven suspension bridges were swept away, thousands of cattle drowned, and agricultural land devastated and buried in sand. A land of rivers, Arunachal is a powerhouse of hydro-energy with the capacity to generate 38,000 MW of hydro-electric power. However, with the state being in a high risk seismic zone, there are fears that mega hydro-electric projects come with a huge risk, and the danger of permanent destruction of unique ecosystems.

The immediate cause of the sudden flood has drawn considerable speculation, especially as the summer rains had not been unnaturally heavy. The Siang river remains unpredictable and only scientists and seismologists can ascertain the cause for this type of calamity as the answer may lie beyond the international border in some unknown catchment area.

The Siang river in Pasighat.

5.

IN THE FOOTSTEPS OF THE GREAT RIMPOCHE

The Land of Pilgrimage and Prayer

Among the Monpa and Sherdukpen tribes of the Tawang and West Kameng districts, *Lopon Rimpoche* is the local name for the Indian monk Padmasambhava, who is believed to have established Buddhism in this area sometime in the eighth century. Following the road to the district headquarters of Bomdila, one is struck by the air of worship and prayer. A pathway of prayer flags flutters in the cold, clear air.

and moon suspended over the eternal wheel. Following the Tibetan calendar, these are erected after the completion of every twelve-year cycle. A *rimpoche* (reincarnate lama) is consulted and according to the year of birth, a particular mantra and type of flag is prescribed. The main flag is colour coded according to the corresponding zodiac sign, and to these are attached strips of cloth:

Blue for the sky and water,
White for the clouds,
Red for fire,
Green for living things, trees and plants,
Yellow for earth.

The other types of prayer flags are the 'man-per', derived from the word *maa-ne,* as in the holy incantation *Om Maane Padme Hum,* and *per*, which means 'a block print'. Hence a 'man-per' is a prayer flag printed with a particular mantra. *Sangfan* is another type of prayer flag that is brought to a place where a ceremony or ritual is being observed, while *cheyfan* are the strips of cotton or rice paper that are tied to shrubs and trees for the wind to disperse the inscribed prayers and wishes in every direction.

West Kameng is devoutly Buddhist and daily life is closely interwoven with religious practice. Among the Monpa and Sherdukpen, seven and nine places, respectively, are considered to have become hallowed by the Padmasambhava's visit. These are places where the great Master is believed to have sat in meditation, leaving impressions of his presence that the locals revere and cherish to this day.

His Holiness the Dalai Lama during his visit to the Thubsung Dhargyeling Monastery in Dirang in 2017.

Beyond the soft rain and mist of Bomdila, on the road to Tawang lies the fortress town of Dirang-Dzong. The old fort is a four-storeyed structure that was built in 1831 to function as an administrative centre under the direct control of the Tawang monastery. A senior monk, called a *dzongpen,* whose main duty was to collect taxes for the monastery, was despatched to run it. Legend has it that the construction of the fort was fiercely resisted by the men of twelve leading householders of the village who opposed the authority of the Tawang monastery being imposed on the freedom of the people of Dirang. In the ensuing armed struggle, all twelve leaders were brutally killed. Today, the fort stands in the old village as silent testimony to the brave men who fought for the freedom of the Monpas of Dirang. Despite their conversion to Buddhism, many of the Monpas of Dirang still practise the pre-Buddhist Bon religion and perform rituals of the older Nyingmapa Buddhist sect.

In the old gompa (monastery), a black stone measuring some eight by four inches is preserved. It is black and polished except on one side, which is rough and has a few notches on it. The stone is believed to be the petrified heart of a fierce, malevolent spirit who had its haunt in a huge rock in the village until a rimpoche killed it and established Buddhism in the area. The notches are said to be sword marks, and the rough surface is the place where the heart was severed from the body. The landscape is dazzling in its beauty. Dirang is apple orchard country. Nestled amidst hills of blue pine and rhododendron, this hamlet is blessed with mild climate, great scenic beauty and wealth in fruit, flowers, aromatic and medicinal herbs. The Monpas use their land very productively. Men and women toil equally hard in the fields and after the harvest, layers of dry oak leaves are spread on the fallow earth and their animals are allowed to graze at will. Wooden ploughs driven by yaks till the soil. The most common crops are barley, maize, wheat, radish, turnips, beans and cabbage. An emphasis on horticulture has improved and increased apple production while experimental cultivation of kiwi fruit, persimmon and nectarines yield excellent results.

Monks performing the Cham dance.

Near Dirang there are also two *Lish* villages. The Lish are a relatively small community who speak a language quite different from the Monpas they live so close to. They continue to practise pre-Buddhist rituals and are known for their expertise in slate-roof laying, and are often employed by the Monpas for this purpose.

The Legend of Banggajang

At the highest point on the national highway to Tawang, Sela top (4.419 metres), a road forks into a region of wild granite peaks and sacred lakes hidden in the Sela-Banggajang mountain range. Banggajang is the name of a deity whose manifestation is the serene lake known as the lake of the goddess Dorji Phama. A small gompa stands alone in this desolate landscape and devotees flock here during the short season before winter sets in when a lama comes from the Tawang monastery to perform special prayers. Enormous rocks and strangely-shaped stones are decorated with prayer flags and the marks of pilgrims who travel this route braving icy winds and steep climbs in altitudes of 17,000 feet and above. There are many lakes in the area; each one bearing a special attribute, but the most sacred and powerful is believed to be the lake of Dorji Phama. Prayers are granted here and the lake is strewn with offerings of coins, gold and the ceremonial scarf *(khata)*. There is a belief that those whom the goddess favours can see the reflections of burning lamps or other auspicious signs, like banners of prayer flags in its waters.

The Tawang Monastery.

In the main prayer hall of the Tawang Monastery.

Tawang Monastery

According to local legend, more than 400 years ago, a great monk, Lodre Gyatso, or Mera Lama as he is popularly known, travelled to this area in search of a site for a new monastery as a centre for the reformist 'Yellow Hat' or Gelugpa sect of Mahayana Buddhism. On a hill near Tawang, he sat down to pray for guidance. When he looked around again he found that his horse had wandered off, and following its footprints, he came upon the palace of one of the Tawang kings, Gyalpo Kala Wangbu. He at once perceived this as a divine sign, that this was to be the chosen site. In another version, the horse, on reaching the present site of the monastery, refused to go any further and instead began to paw the earth with his feet. In recognition of the part played by the horse that led him to the site, Mera Lama called the chosen place *Ta-Wang, (ta*—horse, *wang*—chosen). The full name of the monastery is Tawang Ganzen Namgye Lhacheh, meaning 'the celestial paradise of the divine site chosen by a horse'.[1] There is no accurate data in the monastery records today regarding the actual date of construction of the Tawang monastery, but it is placed at sometime between 1643 and 1647.

Young trainee monks.

In the Tibetan month of *dawa-chukjipa* (on dates corresponding roughly to 10-12 January) the chanting of men and the long echo of trumpets herald the first day's ritual of the *Torgya* festival performed in the Tawang monastery every year. Every third year Torgya is celebrated on a grand scale and is called Dungyur. At this time a special ritual called the *Mani Dum Drub* is conducted by monks. Devotees from all over the country and Bhutan, Sikkim and Nepal crowd the ancient courtyards to receive blessings and to watch the famous monastic dances and pantomime dramas that depict the triumph of good over evil, and how the soul is received into the other world after death. These mask dances are an ancient tradition and the masks for these performances are more than an object; they are regarded as living characters, be it human, animal or bird. Supernatural power is vested

Monks with Tibetan horns.

in the mask through a ritual of consecration called *ramnye,* performed by a lama, after which the mask or any other image becomes a sacred object of worship; so people other than the dancers generally hesitate to handle the masks, fearing that some ill may befall them.

At a distance of 20 km beyond Tawang towards the international border is Pangkang Teng Tso (lake) at an altitude of 3,500 m. Forests of fir surround the lake. The area is a good habitat for migratory birds and high-altitude animals. Not far from this lake is the beautiful Tak-Tsang gompa, revered as one of the sites that the great Master visited, dating back to the eighth century. A tiger is said to have accompanied him here, hence *tak*—tiger, *tsang*—place. The footprints of the great Master and his horse are also imprinted on a rock and the walls of the gompa were once adorned with beautiful frescoes, which however, have faded with neglect and time.

A Buddhist nun lighting lamps.

6.

GIFTS OF THE GODS

The Inheritance of Man

In the beginning, there was no moon but two suns who gave heat and light. *Epanja* was the father of the suns and their mother was *Lanbbai.*

One day, the younger of the two suns said, 'Brother, why should we not burn the earth with our great heat?' The elder brother replied that it would be wrong to do so and that in any case his brother's body was too small for it; but the younger brother took no notice. He left home, went to the middle of the sky and began to pour his heat upon the earth. As a result grass and trees dried up and the men working in the fields began to die. Even the houses could not give shelter to the wives and children. Animals

wandered about searching for shade and water, but rivers and streams had dried up too. When Anya, the great god saw the suffering of the earth and the living creatures on it, he called the gods of the sky for a meeting. They decided to send someone to talk to the elder sun, but none of them knew the way to his home.

So Anya said, 'First go in an easterly direction until you reach a place where two rivers meet. Then you must go through Laliya and many other villages until you reach the gate of the sun's house.' One of the gods suggested some rice beer, but Anya said that they should take pigs and fowl and birds, and keep the rice beer for the Mishmis. That is why the Mishmis worship the sun with fowl and birds whenever it is necessary, and drink the rice beer.

Anya's messenger reached the elder sun and offered his presents. The elder sun received him hospitably but when he heard the story of misery caused to the people of earth by his younger brother, he was filled with anger. Seizing the younger sun, he threw him into a pool of mud. Ever since, the younger sun has not dared to go into the sky so long as his elder brother is present. He only comes out when the elder, greater sun goes to rest. As a result of being thrown into the pool of mud, the younger sun grew pale and the marks of the mud may still be seen on his face. The elder sun gave the messenger a silkworm so that men could weave garments from it, and a white jewel for their necklaces. He said to the Mishmis, 'I will always be in the stones as Madulalaya and give you fire.'

In the worship of nature, all the things that man possesses and needs for his daily life are gifts of the gods. When there was no food on earth and the world was covered in rain and wind, man was chosen by the gods to receive knowledge of cultivation and construction of dwellings. Throughout the state all the tribes have their stories to account for the growth of food and gram, and the making of implements for domestic use and hunting and fishing.

A grain of rice is a gift from the underworld granary of the earth mother, the goddess of grain. It was carried back to man by a faithful dog in the crease of his ear. A goddess who was pleased by the rich offerings made to her whispered the art of weaving to the first man's wife in a dream. Then the woman taught it to her daughters using bark fibre and yarn made from the soft feathers of the kite.

The gift of salt was given by the god Mathum Matta in a bamboo tube to the first people who came down from the Himalayan mountains on gold and silver ladders. When the bamboo tube was opened, a girl called Chum-Machan came out, whose body was made entirely of salt.

A Tagin man with pipe.

Bori girls.

The first tobacco plant grew out of the grave of a dead girl. Similarly, the opium poppy grew out of the body of a beautiful girl who died of weariness of too many contending lovers. Her disappointed lovers, who could not enjoy her in life, can now divide and use the fruits of her body. In another story, a variation makes the opium poppy grow out of the body of a lonely girl whom nobody loved but whose death made all men desire her. The opium poppy *(Papaver Somniferum)* is grown in small clearings of 100 sq. metres to fields of 15 acres. It is popular among the Khampti, Tangsa, Wancho, Mishmi and some Adi tribes. It is traditionally smoked in pipes, ranging from simple bamboo to elaborately carved wooden pipes of the Wanchos and the long, decorative silver pipes favoured by the Mishmi women.

The use of opium was generally restricted to domestic consumption by the older generation, and as a cure for numerous ailments. But today the dangers of addiction among the young and the cultivation of poppy for economic returns has become a reality. According to the Customs and Narcotics Control Bureau, the opium poppy came to the hills from Assam where it was introduced in the seventeenth century by the troops fighting for the Mughals against the Ahoms. From 1617 to 1672, more than 17 battles were fought and the troops in the Mughal camp were given a daily ration of opium to make them fight better and withstand the rigours of war. This addiction gradually spread to the neighbouring tribes of the Khamptis, Mishmis, Adis, Singpho, Nocte and Wanchos living in the border areas close to Assam. Today, almost every village where opium poppy is grown has been located and their fields pinpointed. Considering the proximity of the state to the Golden Triangle of South East Asia, the Central Bureau of Narcotics has taken an unrelenting stand to stamp out illegal cultivation. Since 1988, several teams of Customs officers have fanned out over Arunachal to conduct surveys of opium poppy-producing areas. However, their operations have not been easy.

In the Hayuliang, Hawai and Walong circles of the Anjaw district, village elders (Gaon Buras) gave impassioned speeches and said that opium had been a part of their lives from time immemorial. They said they did not want roads, hospitals, schools and electricity. They were happy without the officers and asked them to return to Delhi from where they had come.[2] In the Maryang and Damro circles of the Upper Siang district, villagers turned quite hostile and showed their displeasure in the sudden interference in village matters by hurling stones at the vehicles of the unwelcome visitors. Nevertheless, the Narcotics Bureau is keen to assist schemes to increase awareness among people to curb addiction and cultivation. In one case, more than 15 lakh plants in 18 acres were destroyed in the Maryang circle.

Mishmi men drinking apong (rice beer).

Apart from the use of opium, the love for rice beer is a tie that binds all the tribes together. It goes by the name of *Opo, O, Apong, Zauu, Marwa, Ara, Chang, Yu* and may be made of rice, millet, barley, or tapioca. In Dibang Valley, a pale, gold brew is made from honeycombs called *yu-ambey*. Everywhere, it is held in high esteem and its origin and use are closely associated with myth and ritual. The fermenting agent *(si-ye)* is the key ingredient on which the success of good rice wine depends. It is a dry mixture of crushed leaves and plants mixed with rice powder, and shaped into large, flat discs or smaller, round biscuits. Its preparation is kept secret and most of the si-ye used in homes today is bought from the markets from those who specialise in making it. Apart from the quality of the fermenting agent, it is believed that the brew has its moods and the making of good rice wine that is potent and pleasing, like any other good wine, is considered to be an art. A house is lucky if its women make good rice beer for it is that essential ingredient of social life that binds friends and relatives together, frees the mind, loosens the tongue and makes people happy.

Making apong.

Rice beer is generally prepared in large quantities and packed in bamboo baskets. These are left undisturbed until the fermentation process is complete when the required portion of mixture is scooped out and filtered. A basket can last for a month or a few days, depending on the drinkers.

An old Hill Miri belief: 'Before rice-beer was invented, life was very dull. Men sat about feeling bored; they had nothing to talk about; they did not hold councils or tell stories or laugh.'

Equal to the Gods—A Story about Rice Beer

An old Arunachal story tells of how once upon a time only the gods knew how to make rice beer. They kept this a secret from man because they felt that once he attained this knowledge man would become equal to the gods. It so happened that in those days certain spirits had human forms, and a spirit, Takar Idu, had a pretty daughter called Idu Duming. Both had human forms. Tapu Taleng, who was a spirit in bird form, wanted to marry the girl. He gave her parents a lot of beer and meat and they were pleased and agreed to the match. However, Idu Duming objected to marrying a bird and refused to go to him. This angered Tapu Taleng and one day, when she was bathing alone in a stream, he flew down and killed her. This led to a feud between the two families.

One day, when Takar Idu and his clan were mourning their dead, a man appeared. His name was Nine Nerung and he offered to destroy their enemies in exchange for anything he wanted from Takar Idu. Takar agreed. Nine Nerung killed the spirit birds and when the time came he called on Takar Idu to claim his reward. Takar Idu, however, was drinking with his clansmen and had completely forgotten him. Day and night the feast went on and Nine Nerung sat in the basement feeling cold, tired and annoyed. A few drops of rice beer fell through the floor on to his hands and when he licked it, he liked the taste so much that he resolved to ask for it as his reward.

Finally, Takar Idu offered him beads, mithuns, pigs, valuable dishes, everything he had. But Nine Nerung said, 'None of these are any good to me. All I want is the secret of the stuff you were drinking last night.' They were about to give it to him when Takar Idu said, 'We are spirits. He is only a man. If men get beer they will be equal to the gods.' So he wrapped up the ferment for beer in a leaf parcel and said. 'We give you this on one condition, that you go to the House of the Winds and open it there.'

Nine Nerung agreed and took his parcel to the House of the Winds, but when he opened it, the winds carried the ferment and leaves away. Some of the ferment fell on trees and their fruit has ever since been sweet. As Nine Nerung went weeping to find his prize, he met Rat on the way. He told him his trouble and Rat said, 'If I find it for you, what will you give me?' 'Anything you want,' said the man. Rat found the leaves on which there was a little ferment. Nine Nerung took them home and made rice beer, but forgot all about Rat. Ever since, rats have looked on men as their enemies and do all they can to spoil their crops and damage anything they have.[2]

It is said that the first grain of rice came to man from the goddess of grain, who lives in the underworld. It was carried by the faithful dog in the 'pocket' of his ears. At first, man cultivated the seed in a spot by his hearth. In time, he learned to till the soil outside and spread his harvest.

7.
LEGENDS OF LOVE

Sleep and Love

Originally men did not sleep but worked day and night. The spirits of the mountains and the spirits of the rivers did not like this. They went to Sitking Kedeng, a powerful spirit of the underworld, and said, 'If these people work so much, they will spoil our hills and we will have nowhere to live.' Sitking Kedeng replied, 'Don't worry, I'll see to it.' Now the spirits of night, male and female, came into being far below the surface of the earth. They grew up and married each other and had many children, boys and girls, and built a large village, for they were just like human beings.

One night, the spirit boys and girls went to the human village, caught the souls of the boys and girls and took them away. After that, people began to sleep. The spirit girls have a great dormitory (*rasheng*), where they take the kidnapped souls of human boys and make them dance, and the spirit boys take the souls of human girls and marry them. In the morning, everyone goes back to their home.[1]

Above and below: Stone sculptures found in the excavations at Malinithan.

Love is also a recurring theme in these hills. Beginning with the stories of creation and how earth and sky were lovers, love legends drawn from obscure myths and others based on historical fact form the heritage of these hills. There are hidden stories of love inscribed on rocks and pillars of ruined temples and forts slowly being unearthed across the state. Near the town of Roing in Lower Dibang Valley district are the remains of the brick fortress of Bhishmaknagar. According to local legend this was the palace of King Bhishmak who figures in the Mahabharata and Kalika Puranas as the king of Kaundilya. Near these ruins flows the Kundil river. The Idu people here have an emotional attachment to the legend of Bhishmak and believe that once upon a time Lord Krishna had come to this land to rescue the daughter of the king, Princess Rukmini, and married her. The Idu believe that Rukmini was a daughter of the hills and songs are still sung today glorifying the Krishna-Rukmini legend.

Further west, where the hills descend into the plains, another place associated with the Krishna legend has been revealed by archaeological excavations. Malinithan is situated in West Siang District and it is believed that Krishna and Rukmini rested here on their way to Dwaraka from Bhismak. They were received by Shiva and his consort Durga (Parvati) as guests and offered garlands of the choicest flowers. At this, Krishna, in praise, addressed Durga as 'Malini' ('mistress of the garden') and from then on the place came to be known as 'Malinithan' or 'Malinisthan' (the abode of Malini).

Image of an Apsara in Malinithan.

The alluvial soil and the elephant grass covering the open plain around it suggest that Malinithan might have also once stood on the bank of a river, probably a tributary of the Brahmaputra or the Brahmaputra itself, before it changed course. Today there is no trace of any river flowing near it except for a gully that comes to life during the monsoon rains.

Tai Bida and the Lake

A tale of love and loss is also associated with the Gyakar Sinyi Lake in the state capital, Itanagar. The lake, fed by underground mountain streams, is deep and calm, and surrounded by enormous trees, bamboo and giant ferns. Legend has it that a man named Tai Bida was once hunting in these forests when he came upon a solitary mithun calf. Tai Bida was astonished to meet this calf who started crying when it saw Tai Bida. He brought the calf home and brought her up with great care and devotion. Since then Tai Bida's fortunes changed and he became the wealthiest man of the area. The mithun bred and multiplied, and Tai Bida married and acquired property and precious beads in exchange for his mithuns.

Time passed and the mithun grew old. Tai Bida was also an old man now, with many wives and children. One day his eldest wife fell ill and a priest *(nyub),* was called to find out the cause of illness. The nyub advised a ritual sacrifice and Tai Bida decided to sacrifice the old mother mithun who had brought him so much prosperity and development. That night Tai Bida had a dream. He saw the old mithun transformed into a woman who was weeping and singing a song called *nyem habnam* that is the traditional song of farewell for a bride who is leaving her home. She cried that when she had given him so much happiness and prosperity he had kept her well fed and warm, but now that he was bent on killing her, who would look after her motherless sons and daughters?

The Mithun, an auspicious animal in Arunachal.

When Tai Bida woke, a great storm was blowing. He heard the old mithun weeping and when he came out he saw that the mother mithun was indeed weeping and a number of mithuns had gathered around her. The rope which had bound her had been beautifully untied without any damage and the old mithun began walking away from him. All the other mithuns followed her and Tai Bida could not stop them. Tai Bida called his relatives and they followed the footprints of the mithuns, which led to Gyakar Sinyi Lake. One by one, all the mithuns had stepped into the waters and disappeared, leaving only hundreds of footprints around the lake. Today it is believed the track followed by the mithuns and the stone on which Bida sat repenting his deed can still be seen on Horo hill above the lake.

In Nyishi belief, the mithun (Seenyi) and woman (Beenyi) are born of the same mother. Seenyi is the elder sister and Beenyi the younger one. The sisters had many competitions between them and one of these was a swimming competition in a lake. During the competition Seenyi's loud sneezing frightened Beenyi who was in danger of drowning. She cried out and was rescued by her husband. Thus, Beenyi was defeated in the competition by the mithun. Therefore, traditionally, a woman given in marriage is paid for in mithuns as bride price in Nyishi society.[2]

Ocean of Melodious Purity

'White crane!
Lend me your wings.
I will not fly far
From Lithang, I shall return.'
(Song of the Sixth Dalai Lama)[3]

The Sixth Dalai Lama, Tsangyang Gyatso.

According to the history of Tibet, the sixth Dalai Lama, Tsangyang Gyatso, was born in an area south of Tibet, in the land of Mon. The place is Urgelling, in Tawang, where an old monastery still stands, rebuilt by the local people after it was destroyed by Mongol warriors in the seventeenth century. The Urgelling monastery is one of the three oldest monasteries in the Tawang area and is believed to have been established sometime in the twelfth century as a seat of the Nyingmapa sect of Buddhism (the Red Hats), which held sway before it was overtaken by the reformist Gelugpa sect introduced by Mera Lama, the founder of Tawang monastery in the seventeenth century.

After the construction of the Tawang monastery, Mera Lama returned to Lhasa to convey the good news to the fifth Dalai Lama (also addressed as the Great Fifth), and begged him to pay a visit to the monastery. The Dalai Lama was unable to visit the monastery then but he promised to visit it later. The local people believe that in order to redeem his promise, the Dalai Lama had his sixth rebirth in the person of Tsangyang Gyatso (1683–1706) in Urgelling, Tawang.

Urgelling Gompa.

Tsangyang Gyatso was the son of Lama Rigdzin Tashi, of Urgelling and Tsewang Lhamo, a Monpa girl from the hamlet of Berkhar. Owing to the concealment of the death of the fifth Dalai Lama in 1682, during the period of turmoil under the Manchu empire, the young Gyatso was not recognised as the reincarnation of the Great Fifth until he was ten years old. A secret search was conducted for his reincarnation and in 1685 a report reached the senior monks at the Potala that a three-year-old boy from the Monyul (Tawang) area seemed to be the likely candidate. The child reincarnation and his mother were transferred to Tsona in Tibet and in 1697 secretly taken from Tsona to Nakartse where Tsangyang was educated by appointed teachers, but it was years later that the discovery of the new Dalai Lama was announced. Consequently, he missed out on the strict upbringing and spiritual training of Tibetan Lamaism, and on being enthroned at the Potala in October 1697, he chose instead to practise archery with his friends and spend the day composing verse and love songs.

'It snowed at dusk
When I searched for my sweetheart.
Now the secret cannot be kept;
In the snow my footprints remain.'[4]

While he was a child in the Tawang area, Tsangyang is said to have magically left his footprints on stone and inscribed mystic writings on the rocks with his bare fingers. Visitors to the Urgelling gompa can still see these writings attributed to him. A rock bearing his footprint, about five miles from Tawang where he turned to look at the Tawang monastery for the last time is called *Lama-jabjeih.* A big tree of the species known locally as Chendongseng, located near the gate of the gompa is believed to have grown out of his staff when he planted it there on his departure for Lhasa, saying he would see it again when he returned.

In 1706, Tsangyang Gyatso was taken away by Mongol soldiers from the Potala to China, and was never seen again. In the following years a campaign was carried out to destroy Nyingmapa gompas and erase all traces of the enigmatic Dalai Lama. The double-storeyed temple and pillared assembly hall in Urgelling was destroyed in a raid by the Mongol warrior Sokpa Jamkhar. During this time all the scriptures and sacred objects were handed over to Tawang monastery.

Whatever controversies later historians and scholars see in his life and times, a deep religious loyalty and affection for Tsangyang Gyatso, the 'Ocean of Melodious Purity', still abides in the hearts of the people here. In this land of pilgrimage and prayer, the poignant cry of the rebel Dalai Lama echoes across the vast beauty of mountain and sky.

'In love with the lake
The swan longs to stay
the ice covers the lake
And the swan flies with no regrets'[5].

Sela Lake.

8.

THE WAY OF DONYI-POLO

Looking Through the Sun, Peeping Through the Moon

Among the tribes collectively known as the Tam group, the Donyi-Polo faith is based on Donyi—the sun, and Polo—the moon. They are the symbolic powers through which the supreme spiritual being is manifested. This practice holds that all life is sacred and that the universal spirit resides in every being, in rocks and stones and trees. It is a way of life that involves a close and harmonious relationship between man and the natural world. When a person is just, kind, honest, he is called a Donyi-Polo Ami (a good man). On a number of occasions, in calamity and distress, Donyi-Polo is invoked as a way of ascertaining the truth. Here the Sun is female, addressed as 'Oh mother, the sun shall hear! (*Ane Donyi kalangka!*)'.

The sun and moon represent the all-seeing, omnipresent, universal spirit whose light shines on all equally, and just as the sun and moon are in continuous existence, so also are truth, justice and compassion. In its original concept, the Donyi-Polo faith is an attempt to give meaning to life through intellectual and ideological pursuit based on nature. 'It has no prophets and preachers. It is an evolutionary outcome of human faith. Truth is the essence of it.'[1]

The Role of Memory

Ngitomem atbito, soyolo atbito,
Dolila dosuto, dolila dosuto
Doyingem dosuto ngo.
Sedikem atbito, soyolo atbito
Doila dosuto, dolila dosuto,
Ngitomem dosuto ng!'

('All the words were written
They were written on dried skin
All the songs were written
They were written on dried skin,
But I was hungry, I was hungry
I ate the story. Alas!
I, myself, have eaten all the stories.'[2])

Galo women at the Bascon festival.

The Donyi-Polo faith is characterized by special narrative songs that recount the creation of the world, the birth of man, and all the gods and goddesses that surround him. Among the Galo, this is expressed through the *Nyibo Agom* (poetic language of the priest). There are two categories of priest, the Gumin Nyibo, and the Nyigre Nyibo who fall into a trance and converse with the spirits. It is believed spiritual attendants known as Doyi-lulu or Talo-tanya guide the Nyibo when he is in a trance.

The Adi spiritual and mythological belief is also expressed through narrative songs called *Aabangs,* which are chanted by the shaman priest or *miri.* Aabangs are narrated in an archaic language that is not widely understood these days, but to watch a miri in full flow when he is chanting is to feel the power of words; words that are old and magical, conjuring up vast spaces where man wandered alone and struggled with the spirits before he received knowledge from the gods. The Aabangs explain the reason for the tribes' particular beliefs and remind one of the names and places of all the gods and spirits while instructing the community on how to conduct their rituals for specific festivals and community endeavours.

The miri.

The Legend of the Miri

There are different categories of priests among the tribes and the highest priests possess great supernatural and spiritual powers that are not hereditary. All sacrificial rituals are conducted by priests, whose origin is compared to the birth of the great mountains, the tiger and the snake, wind and water, while their supernatural powers are the blessings of the mighty sun. The qualities of a high priest are inborn and are recognized through the performance of unbelievable ritualistic feats.

Tapu war dance.

A famous priest of the West Siang district, the late Kachi Yomcha, could transmogrify into a tiger *(homen rinam)*. His powers were so great that people were afraid to take his name at night or when they were in the forest. During the middle years of his priesthood, he created two brass images of a female goddess whom he called Topo Go-ne after a legendary woman who was engulfed by a rock when she was resting on it during her marriage journey. The images were seen by many people and were originally kept in a box. Members of the priest's family said they used to hear them jump at night. Today, only one image remains. According to one account, when the great priest was asked about the missing image, he said that it had turned into a malevolent spirit, and whenever a child died, blood appeared on the mouth of the image. So the great priest, after sacrificing a white cock, buried the malevolent image under a rock in the deep jungle. Till date, the location of the missing image remains unknown.

The Idu of Dibang valley have two classes of shaman priests—the Igu Meme who presides at a wide variety of ceremonies and the Igu-A, who is more of a trainee concerned with rituals to ascertain the cause and cure of disease. Every priest has a tutelary spirit and during a trance, the Igu is helped by his tutelary spirit who guides him along the right course. The tutelary spirit of a male shaman is generally male, but occasionally, he may have a female tutelary. On the other hand the tutelary spirit of a female shaman is always male. A person destined to become a priest usually receives signs in a dream. He then goes into the forest and lives alone for several days, where he falls into a trance and his soul travels to the spirit world. He lives with them for a long time and finds his tutelary spirit from whom he learns the knowledge of spirits.

Ponung, the harvest dance.

In these hills man is surrounded by a host of gods and spirits. Some of them live in the underworld. Some have their permanent home on earth, some in the air and some in human dwellings. There are spirits of fire, sky, lightning, deep gorges, snakes, and murder and feuds. On the other hand there are guardian spirits of the east, of the west and north and upper streams, and deities of protection, children, good crops, cattle and wealth. Through the medium of the priest there is a mysterious communion with the natural world. The priest invokes his tutelary spirit to come to his aid and identify which particular spirit is responsible for a misfortune. Following this a number of sacrificial offerings are made to ward off the cause of illness or disaster and obtain blessings and kindness from other powerful spirits. Everyone participates in these rites and observes the rites and taboos laid down for the shaman that has been conveyed to him through his tutelary spirit, or as a direct sign from a supreme deity, so that man may live in security and peace.

According to the tenets of Donyi-Polo belief, 'in the spiritual and transcendent meaning this supreme power is omnipresent, omniscient and omnipotent, that is, ever vigilant, which the Adis call: *"Donyi Mikmi Seri, Polo Migo Sero"*[3]. In recent years a movement to revive the institution of priesthood and uphold indigenous beliefs has gained momentum in the state. The Donyi-Polo Yelam Kebang, a socio-religious organisation was founded in Pasighat in 1986 with 'the spirit of achieving a new testament of faith and practice.'

This organisation today has a wide following in the state and has, to a certain extent, succeeded in institutionalising the Donyi-Polo faith through the practice of conducting services in houses of worship called 'Donyi-Polo dere' or Gangging. New hymns have been composed and the oral tradition is being documented and compiled through various study groups to rediscover the philosophy of Donyi-Polo,[4] while ceremonial performances like the lighting of incense and the tying of a sacred thread made from a creeper known locally as *ridin* have been introduced.

At the same time, an association of priests, called the Arunachal Pradesh All Nyibus' Welfare Association (APANWA) was formed, bringing traditional priests variously known as nyibo, nyub, miri, igu, *gwak,* and *kambring* among the different tribes, under one umbrella. A move towards cultural renaissance through spiritual centres like the Nyedar Namlo of the Nyishi, the Kargu Gangin of the Galo, and the Medar Nello of the Apa Tani has gained momentum and the Indigenous Faith and Cultural Society of Arunachal Pradesh (IFCSAP) was formed in 1999. The last day of every year (31 December) is recognised as Indigenous Faith[5] day with Donyi-Polo of the Tani group, Intaya of the Idu Mishmi, and Rang Frah in Changlang district. At this time, families exchange greetings and gifts of food, and gather together to rediscover and revive indigenous faith as a life system that provided man with physical and spiritual resources to survive in a hard, often hostile terrain through the centuries.

Trophies of animal heads at the entrance to an Adi house.

9.

THE JOY OF LIVING

Dance, Colour, Costume

In the villages the people say, 'We stay here because of the celebrations of spring and summer, the dance and song.'

Here there are no lights. The roads are steep and mountainous and sometimes non-existent. The nearest health centre may be many miles away. Yet, travelling in these remote hills, sitting in the dimness of long huts surrounded by mountains and mist, one is always struck by the eagerness with which visitors are received and how village life is characterized by an air of patience and ancient wisdom.

Mishmis cooking a meal.

When the red flower[1] blooms again, it is time to celebrate the arrival of summer. For many days the men of the village have been absent, travelling deep and wide in the surrounding forests—hunting and laying their traps in preparation for *Unying-Aran,* a festival of the Adis that marks the beginning of the new sowing cycle. This is also the special time when the mithuns return to the villages with their young, whose ears are now marked with the brand of ownership. During such times the true spirit of the land and its people is revived in the celebrations of these remote villagers who have never left their homes, except to walk to their fields. Every joy, every feast and prayer is shared equally by all. The elders are not neglected, and a select portion of meat is always kept reserved for the oldest people in the village. Old men and women forget their aches and pains and join in the celebrations, drinking wine and narrating stories.

From the swirling monastic dances of Tawang in the west to the spectacular warrior dances of the Noctes and Wanchos in the east, the cycle of the seasons is officially celebrated in the great festivals of Torgya, Losar, Chindang, Reh, Ojiyele, Mopin, Mol, Loku, Si-Donyi, Dree, Solung across the state, while many communities still continue to observe these rites in their villages on dates fixed by consensus through the local Council of Elders and through divination by priests.

The Solung festival.

Such occasions are full of gaiety and feelings of kinship as community living is revitalized through the shared store of legends fixed in the collective memory of the tribe, which are now brought to life by the songs of the priests. Almost all tribal belief is tied up with agricultural practices, but even though the festivals are linked to the agricultural cycle, the religious aspect is always present. In the epic songs it is clearly mentioned that the mother goddess and the creator of the universe had advised mankind to observe each festival according to the season meant for it so that man would flourish and enjoy the fruits of the earth bestowed on him by benevolent gods and goddesses.

In Arunachal, there are many festivals celebrated statewide, which, in earlier times, were ritual occasions exclusive to particular communities or clans.

Animal sacrifice is a common ritual in most of the festivals, particularly in the non-Bodhic tribes. This has its roots in the belief that instructions were given to man at the beginning of the world to honour the gods with such sacrifice and offerings. The shaman priest takes centrestage,

The Wanchos.

leading the ritual dance and interceding with the gods for the health, happiness and prosperity of the community. The earth is the producer of food, and rituals are performed accordingly. Rituals are also performed to protect granaries and invoke the goddess of wealth to leave the dark jungle and stay in the granary: '*Paddy and millet I keep here. O! Goddess of wealth! Come O! Stay in the granary, Come, Come!*'[2]

Though the times have changed, festivals are firmly blended with the life of the people as occasion to bring kith and kin together, to share food, offer sacrifice and please the gods. Many of the festivals today are celebrated as mega-events to showcase the state's rich legacy of diverse cultures. In far flung areas the district wise characteristics are maintained with the festival schedule fixed collectively by the villagers, or sometimes by the deputy commissioners of the district.

In all cases the approach of a festival day generates great excitement and preparation. The place for the sacrifice of animals is erected, rice beer is prepared by the basket load, and groups of dancers get ready with dress and ornaments, bells, cowry and conch shells, ivory and brass armbands and metal wristlets, coloured tassels, feathers, cane hoops, and beads and waistbands.

In March-April the Wancho celebrate their most popular festival, Ojiyele, for a period of six to twelve days interspersed with prayer, song and dance. Villagers exchange bamboo tubes of rice beer as a mark of greeting and good will. The start of the festival is usually heralded by the firing of blank shots that add to the noise and merriment as vibrant Wancho dancers make their entry. The Wancho male dancers generally wear a white or pale blue loincloth tucked into a cane waist band. A cane basket decorated with coloured beads and tassels, and fitted with a bell hangs from the waist and the tinkling of bells is the only musical sound. They carry swords with handles decorated with goat's hair dyed red and wear armbands of ivory or polished wood, and necklaces of coins and small beads intricately threaded with anthropomorphic designs and symbols. Ear plugs of wild goat's horns or decorations of red woollen thread are also worn and a red cane helmet complete the headdress, which is decorated with boar tusks and hornbill feathers.

Throughout the year festivals are celebrated by one or other of the tribes. Some of the important festivals are *Solung, Mopin, Losar, Boori Boot, Dree, Nechi Dau, Khan, Rangloh* and *Chaloh Loku, Longte Yullo, Mol, Nyokutn, Ojiyele, Reh, Sunken, Si-Donyi* and *Tamladu,* and dance performances are part and parcel of the celebrations.

Rikhampada dance of the Nyishis.

Among tribes like the Adi, Galo, Nocte and Wancho there are no musical instruments to accompany the dance except for bells and metal discs fitted on a sword that produce a rhythmic beat for the pure chanting of the Ponung dance of the Adi. The other tribes have the gong and cymbals, drum, flute, and the Buddhist Monpa, Khamba and Memba, and Sherdukpen play trumpets, drums, conch shells and cymbals in their dances. There is also the famous log drum of the Nocte and Wancho of Tirap, though this was associated more with war and expeditionary raids against enemy villages.

'*The members of the dormitories have assembled.*
All will come to know by the beating of the drum that we are dancing.
All of you see our dance.
Call all the villagers, we will play the drums' [3]

The Tangsa of Changlang district also play the gong and drum, but the drum is played only during the Mol ceremony observed in June-July, after the sowing of paddy. The drum is perceived as a sacred ritual instrument and among the Lungchang Tangsa sub tribe, one household is selected to be the keeper of the drum for a period of three years. 'For this period the household is called the Nongrumham (nong—drum, rum—to worship, ham—house), i.e., the house where drums are worshipped.'[4] The Sangken festival of the Khampti of Lohit District is an occasion to bathe images of Lord Buddha. Sangken also heralds the New Year and people sprinkle water on each other as a sign of merriment.

Tutsa drummers.

Another important festival is Tamladu celebrated by the Digaru Mishmi tribe. During the festival prayers are offered to the God of Earth and the God of Water for protection against natural calamities. The supreme Lord Jebmalu is worshipped for the welfare of human beings, the standing crops, and domestic animals. The Idus celebrate *Reh* in the month of February. Originally an individual would host a feast to reunite clan members. (Reh means 'to call'.) In these high hills where villages of two or three houses are scattered far and wide, relatives could meet only at such times. A messenger was dispatched carrying a knotted string signifying the number of days to the day of the celebration. The recipient would hang this in a prominent place—like the drying rack over the fireplace—and remove each time-knot as the days passed until he knew it was time to set off to participate in the event. A priest would be summoned to perform the necessary obligations and offer food and sacrifice to the gods. The Idu priests (Igu) are accorded great respect by the people. An Igu has a tutelary spirit that guides him and helps him mediate with unseen malevolent spirits who cause harm to man as well as communicate with benevolent spirits who can protect him and ensure a good harvest, and avert illness, disaster and natural calamities. The Igu carries a special drum stretched with the skin of the Iguana monitor lizard.

The Festival of Solung

Ponung dancers during Solung Lune.

Sotkyang, the ritual sacrifice of a Mithun.

Solung is one of the most important festivals of the Adi tribe. The word Solung is derived from a combination of the last syllables of the words *eso*—mithun, and *alung*—together. From the last syllable of the word Solung is further derived, *Lutor* and *Lune*. Lutor, or Etor, is the first Solung and is observed sometime in the month of June. It is primarily concerned with the welfare of domestic cattle and the mithun in particular. It is also the time when new fencing is erected and the ritual dancers in the festivities are the men of the village. The other Solung Lune, held in September is the female Mother Solung, in which the ritual dance called the *ponung* is performed only by women.

Solung begins with the sacrifice of a mithun that is killed through strangulation on a special platform called a *sotkyang*. According to local belief, mankind was once given a mithun and a pig by Dadi-Somi, the god of animals. The dog, a constant companion of the Adis, started barking on seeing the two new animals and so frightened them away. The Adis went to Dadi-Somi and offered food and drink and the two animals were given back to him on the condition that they should not be frightened, not even while being sacrificed. This is how the origin of sacrifice of the mithun by strangulation is explained.

The Solung festival is about words. The power and magic of words that are old, lyrical, mystical. Its unique feature is the Aabang, which is a feat of story telling in verse performed by the priest (miri), who becomes the guest of honour in the village that has invited him. Young and old flock to the community long house (*moshup*) where the performance is held for three days and nights, though in some villages these are stretched to five days of continuous dancing and story telling.

On the first night, the miri puts on his red *ga-le,* the woven wraparound skirt worn by women. His hair is dressed with an ornament called *dumling,* made of precious beads and carefully strung together with twine. In his hand he carries the long sword (*yoksa*) with metal discs at the hilt that will provide the only music for the dance. The miri begins the chanting and rattles his sword, hopping nimbly to and fro across the bamboo floor. The circle of dancers lifts and sways and repeats the first lines of the song in chorus. The pantheon of gods is recreated and the evolution of animals and the birth of the mithun, offspring of the gods, is recounted in full detail. This is called the *Limir Libom Aabang*.

Every tribe has shamans. This is an Idu Mishmi shaman of the Lower Dibang valley.

The second night is devoted to recounting a long journey in which the miri takes the dancers through unknown villages and across rivers to the distant lands of other tribes. Places and scenes are pointed out by the miri and the history of the tribe is retraced through the remembrance of ordeals encountered and overcome in the routes of migration. This is called *Bedang-Ennam,* literally meaning 'to travel the road'. The dancing begins late in the evening and continues all night. Wide-eyed children stay close to their elders, listening with rapt attention to the amazing stories of gods and spirits, demons and animals, and the struggles of man. Sometimes, an elder might comment loudly if he notes a snag in the narration, to which the miri replies in impromptu verse. Young girls who participate in the ponung are instructed not to fall asleep or miss a step as such an act spells misfortune or early death. The journey is a long one and the dancer must remain steadfast and not lag behind, otherwise her soul might be lost in these travels through the world of men into the kingdom of the underworld.

When the young shoots of paddy are emerald and thrusting up, the last rites of Solung, called *Binnyat,* is performed. This is a symbolic ritual performed only by women who make offerings of rice paste, wine and the blood of a sacrificed animal in the rice fields. A little of the rice paste is smeared on the young shoots and prayers are offered to *Kine-Nane,* the goddess of grain, in gratitude for her gift of paddy to mankind. On their way back to the village, the women also smear their carrying baskets with rice paste.

The *Binnyat Aabang* is the longest of the epic songs and is recounted as the final part of the Solung Aabang. It tells the story of how grain came to man. The miri begins his narration with the mythical land of the beautiful and divine land of Fish and Stars, called *Engo-Takar*. He conjures up the great forests

where the predecessors of man lived and had to eke out a living. He describes how man was assisted by the gods of metallurgy and fire in his efforts to clear the forest for cultivation and settlement. Various fruit-bearing trees, sweet potatoes and yams were sown in the clearings. One day, however, the people of Engo-Takar were aghast to see their fields destroyed and their carefully sown crops uprooted and eaten. They sent the *sik-ke,* a civet-like creature to find out the culprit. The sik-ke hid herself in the bushes and cast a sharp eye on the field, where she saw a gigantic creature, like a wild boar (*gumgong*) appear in the field and start uprooting the tubers. The sik-ke ran back as fast as she could and divulged what she had seen in the field.

Now a problem cropped up. The people of Engo-Takar had no weapons to kill the boar. So they called Nui and Gamro, the renowned hunter brothers of the underworld, for help. The next day, the brothers sent their dog Sanyi into the forest and hid among the foliage. During the hunt, a number of events occurred. A mithun belonging to Dadi-Somi, the god of animals, dashed out. At the same time, the boar ran out and Gamro fired his arrow. However, the arrow did not kill the boar and the animal fled back to the underworld. The dog Sanyi chased the boar valiantly but soon lost the footprints of the animal and also the path back home. Instead, Sanyi stumbled into the abode of Kine-Nane, the earth mother and goddess of grain. The good dog introduced herself and said that she had come from the land of Engo-Takar. The goddess heard the whole story and said that she also was waiting for a representative from that land to send back seeds of grain to the Engo-Takar people. She asked the dog to carry some grain and filled the ear pockets of the faithful dog with paddy.

This is how grain came to the world and this is the reason why the Adis still make these offerings during the Solung festival and offer binnyat to honour Kine-Nane and receive her blessings for a good harvest.

On the last day of Solung, the ceremony of *Taktor* is performed to ward off evil spirits who might be tempted to visit the village in search of the blood of sacrificed animals and who might inflict harm and trouble on man. Bows and arrows tipped with pieces of ginger are hung over the entrance of homes and at the gates leading to the village.

Then the time comes for the miri to depart. All the dancers gather to see him off; he is laden with gilts of meat, rice and wine. Sometimes it is an emotional scene as the dancers weep to see him leave their village, for so many nights they have travelled the long road together. Through the words of the miri they have discovered the world as it was in the beginning and found again a little of what was lost or forgotten in the routine of daily chores. The role of the miri as storyteller is unforgettable and irreplaceable. Travelling great distances, he comes to remind people of the meaning and significance of rituals and restores harmony and understanding between man and invisible gods and spirits, man and the forest, and all the animals that he keeps and encounters.

The Origin of Dance

A long time ago, there were two villages, one on either bank of a big river. There was no bridge so the villagers of one bank could not visit the village of the other bank. Marriages had, therefore, to be arranged within the narrow circle of each village. Many people had to remain unmarried, and as a result, the population began to decline. A monk named Chapjam Wangmu decided to build a bridge over the river to promote social intercourse between the two villages. This, however, proved to be difficult as the material collected for the construction of the bridge by day was taken away by the spirits during the night. So the monk arranged for a pantomime to be performed.

The Aji-Lhamu dance.

When the performance of the pantomime was going on, those spirits came to see it. While they were so engrossed, a group of workers collected the material, constructed the bridge and promptly dedicated it to the gods. After the pantomime was over, the spirits returned, only to find that the bridge had been completed. Since it was dedicated to the gods, they could do no harm to the bridge.

The inhabitants of the two villages started visiting each other, the problem of marriage was solved, and the population of the village began to increase. This is believed to be the origin of the famous *Aji-Lhamu* dance, a swirling pantomime traditionally performed by five dancers wearing ferocious masks representing Gyeli, Nyapa, the chief protagonist, Nyaro, the antagonist and two female characters called Lhamu and Lham. Lhamu is the fairy goddess from the firmament, who later becomes Gyeli's queen.

The Story of Weaving

All the tribes of Arunachal Pradesh produce their own cloth though it is believed that originally people did not wear clothes because they did not know how to weave. Instead, they wore cane hoops and metal discs until the secret of weaving was whispered in a dream by a goddess to the wife of the first man. Weaving is also regarded as a gift from the gods, and there are many stories linked to this art.

An Apa Tani woman weaving.

Among the Apa Tani people, the great weavers of the beautiful Ziro plateau, the story goes that in the remote past, there was nothing except cloud and water until fire was born. Following this, the first man on earth, Abo Tani emerged out of the soil. He was not born in human form and passed through many stages of evolution until he reached the present form. Mythology reveals several epochs when Abo Tani was capable of fighting with gods and deities as he had *Koga-Miiri*, a third eye at the back of the head. He also had *Ludu-Piimi*, or two spikes, one each at the end of the heels. During these earlier epochs he could see everything at once with the help of the third eye and with the help of the two spikes as powerful weapons, Abo Tani battled with gods and goddesses. In this way, he captured almost all the fertile land, the gentle river, the useful trees and plants and chased away all the deities to the mountains and desert regions of the earth. Abo Tani even captured the day and left the night for the spirits and gods during his various stages of evolution. However, it was in the epoch of Mudo Lemba that *pulyeh,* cloth, first came to man. It was made by an industrious lady whose name was Ami Tamang Binyii.

Perhaps the time had come for men to discuss the state of the world and the unending battles of Abo Tani and the spirits over land and territory. Abo Tani's materialistic life was on the rise and spiritual life on earth was waning, until even the gods held a conference and captured Abo Tani. Abo Tani fought for his freedom but was ultimately overcome by the allied forces. His third eye and the spikes on his heels were eliminated and he was cursed to remain on earth under the command of the gods, with his dual nature of both good and evil, during his life span on earth. Access to god was cut off forever till he desired to show himself.

Jilan Pulye motif of the apa tani.

A popular design of flower, elephant and peacock motifs on Sherdukpen and Monpa cloth.

A conference of elders called Buliang was called for the first time and an appropriate cloth to signify the importance of the meeting was called for. Binyii was the first woman to identify the seeds of cotton and she wove a white cloth. But the cloth was rejected and thrown away. A bird, the white eagle, called *Kejee Papuh* picked up the cloth and draped himself in it so he remained white forever.

Two other women—Ami Dumi Tadu and Ami Yami Tamang joined the competition to weave the best cloth but their cloth too found no favour. Time was running out. Binyii roamed in the forest wondering what type of cloth would please the elders. One day she discovered a yellow dye from a tree called '*sankhii*', and an idea struck her. She knew of the red dye of the tamen creeper and mixing this with the new colour, she wove a design that received the approval of the gathering and is today identified as the famous Jilang motif of the Apa Tani.[5]

The Jilang shawl is worn only by the highest shaman. An assistant priest called Jigjiro wears another shawl with blue and red stripes and a white shawl, like the one the eagle picked up is given to men during *miida* or marriage celebrations. It is also believed that the first priest on earth was Dolyang Chajang, the sister of Abo Tani. She learnt the knowledge of priesthood from Charung, the god of knowledge.

Women weaving at the Menchuka Crafts Centre.

In one Mishmi story, the first weaver was a girl named Hambrumai, who was taught the art by the god Matai. She sat by the river and learnt her designs by watching the waves and their ripples. She lay in the forest and gazed up at the branches of trees and flowers and ferns and the leaves of the bamboo, and copied them in her designs. Her work was as beautiful as her face and many boys desired to marry her. In Verrier Elwin's words, 'But one day *Hairum,* the porcupine, saw her cloth and came to steal it from her cave. The entrance was too small for him, so he pushed the rock into the river and the girl was crushed beneath it. Her loom was broken to pieces and carried by the stream to the plains and the people there found it and learnt to weave. The designs turned into butterflies and in the markings on their wings you can still see today the patterns she made.'[6]

In a variant of the story, Hambrumai is a fish called Hambru, who had flowers on her body and lived in the Khamlang river along with a snake of three colours—red, blue, and white—which were reflected in the clouds. One day Hambru was caught in the trap of the orphan boy, Kowonsa. Captivated by the beauty of the fish that he had caught, Kowonsa hid her in a gourd and kept her in his house. The next day, when he returned from work, he found his little hut filled with beautiful cloth patterned with the scales of fish and the markings of a snake. This went on for some time. One day he hid near by and watched in amazement as the fish came out of the gourd and turned into a girl with long hair carrying a loom on which she wove many pieces of cloth. Kowonsa married Hambru and she taught all the women of that place to weave. When they asked her how she learnt the patterns, she told them that when she was a fish in the river she had observed the markings of the snake and copied them in her designs.

One day Kowonsa put some cloth out in the sun and the wind blew it away to other villages. That is how other people learnt to weave. The gods Bronmai and Mollo also went about the world teaching everyone how to weave. After Hambrumai died, they took the sword from her loom and made it into a diamond pattern. This, the Mishmis believe, is why there are so many diamonds on the Mishmi cloth.

A child in an Adi ga-le. The Adis have a legend: Once, there were two suns, who wore ga-les of flaming red and yellow. Theie enemy, the frog, stole the gales, and the suns refused to come out into the sky. The world was dark, until the master craftsman Buisi Ada made them belts of metal discs called beyobs. Among the Adi there are different types of beyobs worn by young and adolescent girls, which are discarded after the birth of their first child.

Unlike in other parts of India, in Arunachal Pradesh, weaving is the exclusive monopoly of women. An exception is the striking black and white war coat of the Idu of Dibang Valley, called the Atondre. The Antondre was originally woven using the fibre of the Mallu plant *(Rhea nivea)* that grows wild in these mountains. The weaving is done on a vertical frame called the *Ang-goh*, and the production of this coat is done by the men of the house. It takes 20 days to a month to weave an Atondre, and its thickness and strength is said to be strong enough to turn an arrow and deflect sword blows.

Both women and men delight in wearing beads.

Almost every household possesses one or two looms and the implements of weaving for the portable loin loom is inherited by women. Weaving is a social activity generally done outdoors on open verandas in full view of every passer-by. Among the Adi tribe the *sumpa,* the batten, made from the inner stem of a wild palm is the prized possession of a weaver and regarded as a weapon for women, equivalent to a sword. It is imbued with magic and sometimes placed by one's bedside to ward off evil spells. The original patterns were simple and straightforward. The weavers' first depictions were of the natural world and the patterns show a highly developed sense of abstract art where zig-zag lines signified the course of a river or a jungle track and the characteristic chevrons and pyramids are outlines of the mountains alongside stripes, squares and bands varying in width and colour. There are also formal arrangements of lines and elaborate patterns of diamond and lozenge shapes. Various designs are identified as the grasshopper's tooth, the scales of a fish, the rainbow, and the diamond 'eye design'. The design and colour varies not only between tribes but also between different villages, and each tribe has its own patterns that are never copied by another tribe.

All the tribes have a great variety of skirts, shawls, bags and jackets for men and women, and a tribe can be recognized by the motifs of its textiles. So great is the importance attached to weaving that it is believed that one of the penalties of death is that it sends you to a place where there are no weavers. Besides weaving there is a rich tradition of metal/alloy ornaments and objects, weapons, and cane and bamboo craftsmanship, especially in the making of hats and helmets. Some of these hats are woven so finely that they are waterproof and can withstand a sword blow. The hats are often decorated with feathers of the Great Indian Hornbill or with boar's tusks. Today, due to environmental concerns, a new headgear using fibreglass in lieu of the traditional hornbill beak has been introduced to simulate the traditional headgear with beaks of the hornbill attached to the upper portion worn by men of the Nyishi tribe.

Weaving a cane basket.

10.

DESTINATION ARUNACHAL

A Rich Land in the East

Land of sunrise. The sharp outline of hills. The river at dawn, green and mysterious...

When the first group of foreign tourists came to the town of Pasighat, two elderly local ladies approached me and whispered, 'Are they Chinese?' They were British and French, but the old ladies were seeing foreigners for the first time. The year was 1992, and the first meeting of the Himalayan Tourism Advisory Board (HIMTAB) was being held in the state. It was decided then that the time had come for Arunachal to open its doors to tourists, both domestic and international.

Since then the state has been concentrating on putting Arunachal on the tourist map. It has been a long, slow, road, but the tourism sector is still the most attractive and viable development option and revenue earner for the state today.

Arunachal's rivers are popular destinations for river rafters and anglers.

In 2001 the state Department of Tourism in collaboration with the Union Tourism ministry organized the Brahmaputra Darshan festival in Lohit district with a three-day programme of river rafting, angling, cultural events and exhibition stalls to commemorate the entire Brahmaputra valley culture which developed along the course of this great river and its three main tributaries—the Lohit, Siang and Dibang. The rivers of Arunachal feed and become the mighty Brahmaputra in the plains of Assam, and these rivers provide a unique environmental world, which gives the state the honour of being one of the greenest parts of the country. In subsequent years, a Siang Darshan festival was held on the banks of the Siang river in Pasighat town to promote the region as a tourist destination, and the Siang River festival has become a regular feature in Aalo, West Siang district.

Girls in white yak-hair caps at the Buddh Mahotsav.

At the same time, Tawang hosts the annual Buddh Mahotsav, another big event to woo visitors and also to celebrate the state's legacy of cultural diversity and its colourful and distinct way of life. Arunachal Pradesh may have been slow to open its doors to external influence, but this, in a way has served to preserve its land and its people. In terms of its unique cultural variety, scenic beauty and its unexplored ecological wealth, Arunachal has few rivals.

The Jairampur Graves

In February 1998 a war cemetery was discovered in a thickly wooded forest reserve near Jairampur in Changlang district of Arunachal Pradesh. An epitaph written in Chinese letters found at the site confirmed that the graves were of the officers and men of the 2nd Company of the Independent Engineers of the Chinese army stationed in India during the Second World War.

One epitaph reads: *Major Hsiao Chu Ching, Company Commander of 2nd Company, 2nd Battalion of 10th Regiment, Independent Engineers of Chinese army. Born: July 1913, at Wei Country of Hopeh province. Died: December, 1943.*

What happened here? How did so many soldiers die? What is the story of these men? According to archival sources the site is the World War II cemetery of the famous Y Force of Chinese soldiers who were to push into northern Burma (Myanmar) from the eastern sector and join the American-trained X Force to crush the Japanese forces in Burma and stop their entry into India. The neat rows of simple brick graves are laid out on slightly elevated land between the Namchik river and a historic road known as the Stilwell Road that runs through this territory before cutting into Myanmar. There are about a thousand graves in this area. Each grave measures 1.28 metres x 2.20 metres. All four sides of each grave are constructed with good quality bricks and the top is covered with a concrete slab.

While the war raged in Europe this Asian frontier was a remote and distant theatre of the war. The thick vegetation has kept the graves hidden from view all these years and only time and erosion have unearthed them, so unexpectedly resurrecting the memory of a war fought at our doorstep and a famous road that evokes so much of our legendary past.

Stilwell Road

'*Too much Rain. Too much mud. Too much malaria!*'
(General Lewis A. Pick)

image of the Stilwell Road displayed in the Coal Heritage Park and Museum in Margherita, Assam.

More than half a century later the words of the general still ring true. In this part of the world that Pick was talking about, there is still enough rain to submerge mountains, enough mud to swallow villages, enough cases of malaria. And running through all this mud and rain and the jungle swarming with mosquitoes is the famous Stilwell Road—still there, emerging out of the past like a shadowy image full of ghosts and stories, and also full of promise as a tantalizing corridor into Myanmar and a gateway to Asia via the north-east region of the country. The nation's 'Look East Policy' has added a new meaning to all this. All these years the historic road has been lying abandoned, pointed out as a route from where insurgent groups crossed borders for arms and training in jungle camps hidden in this no-man's land. However, the inauguration of a Border Trade Centre that leads to this famous road, in Nampong, Changlang district, opened the way for border trade between India and Myanmar.

American GIs in Ledo, the starting point of the Stilwell Road, in 1944.

Nampong is the famous last stop before the mysterious road veers up to the Pangsau Pass on the crest of the Patkoi hills and into Myanmar, curling like a giant serpent across three countries from Ledo in Assam, through Arunachal Pradesh, into Myanmar and on to Kunming in the Chinese province of Yunan.

The road was named after General Joseph Warren Stilwell, Deputy Supreme Commander of the Allied Forces South East Asia Command (SEAC) during World War II. Lord Louis Mountbatten was the Supreme Commander of SEAC with its headquarters at Kandy in Ceylon (Sri Lanka). In 1937 when Japanese forces laid a sea blockade on China and captured Rangoon in March 1942, vital support links for Chiang Kai-Shek's Nationalist Kuomintang Army who were fighting the Japanese in western China were cut off. The post-World War I, Burma Road running from Kunming to Lashio in Burma was severed and it became imperative to devise an alternative route. The plan for the construction of an all-weather road, originally christened the Ledo road, was made in February 1942. The idea was to link up the Ledo road with the old Burma road at Mongyu junction in Burma. The American General Lewis A. Pick was the man selected to be chief engineer in charge.

Work began from both the Kunming and the Ledo sides almost simultaneously in April 1942. According to historical data the road follows the alignment of the ancient trail used by the great Sukhapa who established the Ahom kingdom in Assam, as well as the caravan routes of Marco Polo and Genghis Khan in the twelfth and thirteenth centuries. An interesting landmark on this road is a small gate at the 663rd milestone that apparently marks the spot used for changing of couriers on the communication system established by Genghis Khan. Centuries later, the effort required to keep communication lines open for besieged Chinese troops through the Stilwell road was staggering. The road stretches 1,726 km going over mountains, plunging into gorges and crossing ten major rivers and 155 smaller streams. Engineers moved 13,500,000 cubic yards of earth to build this road, which is enough earth to build a wall three feet wide and ten feet high from New York to San Francisco. Thousands of cubic yards of gravel were raked from river beds to surface the road and a million board feet of lumber and pilings were used to fashion a causeway through the swamps of Wazarup and floating bridges over the Irrawaddy river.

A re-paved stretch of the old Stilwell Road between Jairampur and Nampong.

But let us look at this road from our side of the border. Only 61 km of this road lie in Indian Territory, with 30 km in Assam and 31 km in Arunachal Pradesh. In the Arunachal sector a sign over the steel bridge in Nampong had two words: HELL GATE. It was from here that convoys of trucks rumbled away into the dark forest beyond. Today there is little indication of how at the time, forest and sky must have reverberated with the sound of aircraft and trucks carrying men and material to help construct this road by clawing through the jungle and blowing up mountains. American bulldozers were brought in and elephants were also used but they had to be abandoned because they kept slipping in the mud. Countless men died from illness or accident. So high was the toll of human lives that the road was dubbed the 'Man-a-Mile-Road'.

The Patkoi Range seen from the Pangsau pass.

A short drive beyond Pangsau Pass on the Indo-Myanmar border, the land opens out to a view of the 'Lake of No Return'. During the war the lake served as an important landmark for the Allies. The landscape is serene, though it is believed that the marshy area around the lake claimed the lives of over a thousand airmen who died flying this route on 'food drops' and dangerous missions over the Himalayan 'Hump'. They were called the Flying Tigers or 'Hump' pilots, and in 1944 in a period of three months, 'the Tenth Air Force operating out of India flew more than eight thousand sorties and dropped more than 3.7 million pounds of bombs over the Japanese in Burma and India.'[1]

Today archival material is the primary source of information about this road. What remains outside official documentation is the story of hundreds of tribes of the region who were involved in this war effort. Young men from every village were enlisted in the labour corps while many served as porters, guides and informants in ancillary units while engaging in guerrilla warfare.

A young Adi man, Tanmut Yirang of Silluk village in today's East Siang district was awarded the George Medal for bravery during the evacuation from Burma where he rescued a British woman and her baby. The woman was the wife of a pilot and she could not walk due to a leg injury. She was carrying the baby in a bag. First, Yirang ran ahead with the baby and a feeding bottle, fed him some milk and put him up on a tree. Then he ran back and carried the lady. He did this for many miles, running back and forth, until he escorted them to safety in Nampong.[2]

The Stilwell Road was completed in two and a half years. The first overland vehicle convoy from India to Kunming in China left Ledo in January 1945, and the lead truck carried banners that read 'First Convoy Ledo Road'. However, the importance of the road was short-lived as the war ended on 4 August 1945. The famous road fell silent and was confined to history.

In February 1999, following the discovery of the Jairampur graves, the transport ministers of the north-eastern states asked the Union government to restore and declare the Stilwell Road a national highway. The decision was taken in order to boost trade with neighbouring countries and perhaps to restore old corridors of communication between the ethnic and linguistic communities on both sides of the border. However, even today, in the twenty-first century, not many people know about this road. In the Myanmar sector, the road from Myitkyina to Namti and Tanai (Walabum) has been maintained as a motorable all-weather strategic road controlled by the Burmese army since the 1960s, but the portion from the Indian border to the Hukong valley has been a no-man's land for a long time. A National Geographic team was permitted to travel the Ledo road in 2003, but for the most part, the road and the region it traverses remains an inaccessible and mysterious terrain.

Lake of No Return.

In January 2006 an NGO called The Namchik Valley Society for Eco-Tourism & Wildlife Conservation (NSEWC) organized the Pangsau Winter Festival. The venue was Nampong, in the vicinity of the famous road, the World War II cemetery, Hell Gate, the Lake of No Return, and of course, Pangsau Pass. Together with the promotion of local cuisine and the added attraction of ethnic cultural teams from Myanmar, a special feature was the Butterfly India Meet, conducted in association with the Butterfly India group. Since then a segment of the Reserve Forest adjacent to the famous Namdapha Wildlife Sanctuary and Biosphere Reserve has been marked as a Butterfly Conservation Area—one of the first butterfly conservation areas in India.

Around 241 species of butterflies were identified during the fifth edition of the Namdapha Butterfly Meet in 2022. Rare butterflies like the Dragontail, the Red Base Jezebel and Leopard Lacewing were spotted. More than 200 species of moths were observed, including the rare Atlas Moth, the largest moth in the world measuring more than twelve inches across. In a special programme called Breakfast with Butterflies during the meet, schoolchildren trekked happily along narrow jungle paths from Nampong into the tropical rain forest causing a real flutter in the jungles of Arunachal.

The Pangsau Pass Winter Festival is held in Nampong every January. Everything has come together here—the famous road, the lake and the graves of brave soldiers and warriors, the stories of courage and sacrifice, and the hope of communities to reclaim an unwritten history embedded in the past. What began as a small local initiative is now an important event to promote spontaneous cultural dialogue between neighbouring countries, and perhaps on the long road looking east, butterflies will dance again over the Stilwell Road.

The Pressures of Change

The rich wilderness is as fragile as it is beautiful. While the state taps into its tremendous tourism potential and put Arunachal on the swift path to development and modernisation, numerous concerns have come to the fore. With development and the pressing necessity for creating infrastructure, come the associated pitfalls of destruction of the environment and erosion of traditional values.

Road construction outside Itanagar.

Today, Arunachal society stands at the crossroads, confronted with the responsibility of choice. New lifestyles and changing attitudes have encouraged rural migration, while rising unemployment has become a source of discontent and frustration among the youth, and a matter of pressing concern for the state. Apart from its forest resources, Arunachal has no major industry to absorb the growing population of educated youth and professionals. At the same time, communication bottlenecks have proved a major drawback to industrial and economic development.

In the troubled north-east, Arunachal Pradesh used be known as an oasis of peace. This, however, no longer holds true. In the last decades of transition in the post-Independence era, all the states of the North-East region have undergone a dramatic change from a remote, idyllic past into a region that is now referred as ‘conflict zone’. This region faces a conflict of identities that is born of value systems being transformed dramatically, conflicts of political differences leading to the birth of terrorism, increasing demands for ethnic self determination, as well as conflicts inherent in a changing society—between the personal and the political, the state and the Centre, and sometimes, between the individual and organized religion. Since the early days of the North East Frontier Agency (NEFA), Arunachal has seen a lot of change. It became a full-fledged state in 1987 and since then, the world has become smaller. The generation that raised their children in silent, inaccessible villages without electricity can now watch cable TV. The shops are full of new gadgets. The roads are full of automobiles. A new political culture has also drastically changed lifestyles and social outlook.

It is a complex and hard-edged time and it has become essential to find ways to support and interpret the state’s unique cultural heritage and oral traditions, which, in the absence of written records are fading, and which, without proper documentation may be lost forever. In societies where there were no written codes and edicts, the stories handed down from generation to generation provided

Preserving tradition in a time of rapid change.

A woman in Tawang in traditional attire, with a black 'rain hat' made of yak felt.

illumination and explained the basis for many age old customs and practices. This, in a way, has become the backdrop from which an understanding or interpretation of the unwritten past is emerging as the basis for writing the modern history of the state. At the same time, it has also become essential to re-examine customary laws and find out how the modern legal system and the village councils might work together. New crimes that have no precedent in tribal society are increasing, while at the same time, some of the old social practices are no longer valid, especially with regard to the status of women in tribal society.

Tribal people are bound to the land by old and intimate ties. Certain trees were held sacred and it was taboo to cut them down for fear of reprisal from angry spirits. Today, commercial values have swept away these beliefs. As expectations change, so does tribal culture. The Wancho and Nocte warriors no longer feel the need to carve wooden figures that once symbolized the bravery of men in a bygone era. There is also great competition from manufactured goods that now flood the stores while motifs of the old arts are disappearing.

A new generation.

Certainly it is not possible for this generation to return to their hill homes and live as herders and pure agriculturists. A revival of traditional culture will only acquire meaning when the people of Arunachal revitalize the tribal way of life with a new understanding and recognition of its traditional values. It is a matter of hope that with education and awareness, and the dedicated efforts of the concerned departments of state, public leaders, professional groups and the participation of youth, the old stories, ancient patterns and the creative talent of the people of Arunachal could be retained, even though the former ritualistic associations may disappear.

In the words of renowned anthropologist, Dr Verrier Elwin, 'The humblest peasant woman on the frontier makes her contribution to the colourful and varied beauty of the whole picture; every aspiring boy and maiden ripe for love adds to it by making delectable ornaments and decorating head and ear and limbs. Art belongs to the entire people; it has not yet become a monopoly of the few. And because it belongs to them, it: brings them refreshment and happiness ... today there are many grounds for hope. There is a tradition on which to build.'[5]

The north-east of India is Asia in miniature, a region where different races mingle and merge, where India ends and South East Asia begins—and also if we put it this way, where India begins and South East Asia ends. There has also been talk about shared integration for the region in the context of a Greater Asia, looking at geographical location as an opportunity.

A Wancho man resting after a cultural performance.

Indeed, the north-east has been one of the most globalized parts of the subcontinent for well over a century. It was where prosperous tea gardens and companies were set up in the Assam and Barak Valleys, connected to international markets and London. Steamers and ferries took goods and people from as far as Dhaka and Kolkata to Dibrugarh in Upper Assam and back. On the Arunachal Pradesh border, trade among the people living in these areas bordering Tibet, Bhutan and Myanmar has been going on for centuries.

The Himalayas have always attracted pilgrims and holy men, explorers, and adventurers. These mountains are not only a refuge for unique eco-systems and different ethnic groups, but also a treasure house of knowledge and home to little known cultures that offer insights into a world that understands the language spoken by these great forests and mountains.

In these tenacious villages of stone, I have often asked, 'Why do you live here?' And the reply has always been the same. 'We are here because it is our destiny to be here.'

The old men sit on the bamboo platforms of their houses on stilts and gaze out at the wide river. 'Certainly there is change,' they say, 'but what is change after all? It is a moment of transfer, a gift of possibility. People may be leaving the villages now, but you watch, they will come back. Look at the trees! Look at the land! Living here is so much more pleasant.'

There is an old Wancho saying:

'Land is life,
When there is no land
How can a man survive
And what is the use
Of living without land?'

ER
T-GXR

II.

ONCE THERE WAS A LAND

This is how we remember. It is a line of recall for all things, people and places, landscape, geography, and histories swept by time and change.

In post-Independence India, governance was the keyword for a state like Arunachal Pradesh. The aim was to establish administrative centres and step by step open a remote frontier that little was known about. More recently the focus has been on border transport connectivity to bring the north-eastern region closer to the rest of the country. For Arunachal this has meant a slew of transport infrastructure packages from massive hydroelectric schemes and construction of highways to building bridges, airports and railways.

The Dibang River Bridge, which provides all-weather connectivity between Dambuk and Roing.

Today, after decades of debate and setbacks the original concept of a trans-Arunachal Highway has been revived with the ambitious push for a frontier highway of 2,000 km beginning in the west from Mago and running through several districts adjacent to the McMahon line, covering the entire Line of Actual Control (LAC) on the country's border with China, before ending at Vijaynagar in the east near the Myanmar border.

Once a land visited only by explorers and agents of government, the Frontier Highway is touted as a showpiece of the country's biggest and toughest road building projects in a challenging terrain.

Roads open doors. Although not everything is a smooth run yet, a network of inter-district roads branching out like rivulets of a big river have brought far flung villages closer to city centres and to one another. District headquarters—small towns established only for administrative purposes—have turned into thriving hubs of activity catering to individual and collective innovation in business and industrial development. The investment in road connectivity has also opened the way for a number of events in the state's tourism calendar.

For example, the trans Arunachal riders' event, promoted by the Department of Tourism, is a cross country ride from Namsai in the eastern part of the state, riding up to the sunrise village of Dong in Anjaw district, and culminating in Tawang in the far west. This is a ride of a lifetime, travelling through several districts of diverse cultural and geographical landscapes.

'Pedal to Pakke' cycling event.

Other adventure events are the Namdapha-Pangsau-Miao motor cycle tour, a challenging historic circuit covering the Namdapha National Park to Pangsau Pass on the Indo-Myanmar border. The Dirang (West Kameng) Speed festival, and the popular Pedal to Pakke marathon cycling event also draws participants from all over the country.

Namdapha-Pangsau-Miao motorcycle tour.

The Carnival of Change

'A ride on the Pakke Kessang highway is the best!' A taxi driver in Assam tells me.

Not so long ago, the place called Pakke Kessang was a small forest camp where government officers halted for the night in a six-day trek from the Assam border to reach the district headquarters at the town of Seppa in erstwhile Kameng district.

The winds of change are indeed sweeping across the land.

The Pakke river.

Pakke Kessang is now the latest in a line of new districts in the state, created out of the southernmost administrative circles of the East Kameng district, with headquarters at Lemmi, close to the boundary of Papum Pare district and the state capital of Itanagar.

The Pakke Wildlife Sanctuary lies in Pakke Kessang district. The area was initially the Pakhui reserve forest and was renamed Pakke Tiger Reserve when it became the 26th Tiger Reserve under 'Project Tiger' of the National Tiger Conservation Authority. Apart from being home to the three large cats: the Bengal Tiger, the Indian Leopard and the clouded leopard, the tropical semi-evergreen forest harbours a rich diversity of flora and fauna, butterfly, reptile and bird species.

In 2016, Pakke sanctuary won the India Biodiversity Award for its Hornbill Nest Adoption programme of protecting hornbill roost sites. The Reserve has received accolade for its community-based conservation efforts involving civil society, and for the forest department's employment of local youth and village elders as forest watchers in a number of anti-poaching camps.

Scarlet finch.

Capped Langur.

Dendrobium parishii.

Pakke Kessang lies at a juncture where the highway bifurcates to the west leading to the districts of East and West Kameng, with access to Bomdila and Tawang while another connecting road veers up to Ziro and the environs of the beautiful Apa Tani plateau.

Further north, the road leads to the districts of Kra Daadi, Kamle and Kurung Kumey, created with the bifurcation of the Lower Subansiri district under the Arunachal Pradesh Re-organisation of Districts Amendment Act.

In the central belt, two new districts—Leparada (*Lepa*—Centre, *Rada*—'bull's eye') along the southern border with Assam, and Shi-Yomi along the northern border with China—were created in 2018 by dividing the West Siang District.

KYARII SATAM

Arunachal roads may be pounding with the roar of motorcycles and adventure rides but there are hidden places people know nothing about, until stories emerge telling of ancient legends and sacred mountains. Kyarii Satam is one such place, its legend revealed when the tragic news of the missing mountaineer Tapi Mra and his assistant Niku Dao hit the headlines in August 2022.

The initial reaction was that the two men would return. Perhaps they were taking shelter from a storm. Mra, 37, the first mountaineer of the state to conquer Everest in May 2009 was an experienced climber who had scaled a number of peaks in Nepal and Australia, and the Uhuru peak of Mount Kilimanjaro.

Tapi Mra and Tame Bagang.

A mountain boy from Limeking, one of the last Indian villages on the China border in Upper Subansiri district, Mra's childhood dream had always been to scale the world's highest peaks. Kyarii Satam in East Kameng was an alluring challenge. The mountain is a right-angled 7,001 metres snow-capped peak spearing straight up to the sky. This was Mra's fourth attempt to reach the summit. The news of their disappearance had been brought by porters returning from base camp and it was believed that the mountaineer would surely return.

It was a long wait. In the following weeks and months several search and rescue operations by the Indian Army, Airforce, the National Disaster Response Force and state departments were pressed into service to look for the two men. Family members and Mra's mountaineering colleagues along with local villagers mounted determined foot search operations, but nothing of the two men have surfaced till date.

There are certain places—rivers, mountains and forests—that one does not enter without performing the appropriate traditional rituals. Mount Kyarii Satam, for many, is one such place. The mountain is the domain of Brother Kyarii; '*Satam*' is the word for his shield made of bear skin (some say serow skin), describing the black rock face on one side of the mountain that remains bare of snow. According to local legend Brother Kyarii is buried here as it was his last wish to be buried in the mountain so that no other living being could reach him.

The area is remote. The route from the last village to reach base camp is an arduous trek of several days. In 1995, a five-member Indian expedition attempted an ascent of Kyarii Satam over the northeast ridge but the team failed to reach the main summit. The local people here say that when they see the golden peaks of the mountain at sunrise, they can see the shining shield of Brother Kyarii; but they never ventured too close to Kayarii Satam. It is a sacred mountain.

The Open Road

Change happens. 'We want change,' is a common slogan. Societies desire change—a change towards a just and equitable society, political and economic development for an enlightened society; but 'change' when it happens comes with its own dynamics. Arunachal Pradesh today is a go-to destination. Tourism is a big deal, offering a diverse range of adventure, eco-tourism and cultural tours in the backdrop of breathtaking scenery. In November 2022, the state's first domestic airport—Donyi Polo Airport, was inaugurated at Hollongi, 14 km south from Itanagar, the city centre in Papum Pare district. Flight services to Kolkata and Mumbai started by IndiGo airlines began operating on 28 November of the same year, and now flights are booked up well in advance, carrying passengers travelling in, and travelling out.
The new accessibility has brought tremendous change and nowhere is the impact of global world more evident than in the state capital Itanagar where sedate neighbourhoods have changed overnight giving way to bright shops, eateries and hotels.

In this heady atmosphere some changes are totally unforeseen; some others are perceived; however, some are a premonition of hidden danger. One of the gravest threats in this carnival of change is the slow extinction of Arunachal's languages. Scholars say time is of the essence. In the *People's Linguistic Survey of India*, 2017, Arunachal Pradesh was listed as the most linguistically diverse state in India. Every community speaks a different language that is not understood by the other. A few years earlier, the discovery of a completely new, unrecorded language in Arunachal Pradesh received wide media coverage. This was the story of the Koro language, discovered by a team of linguists in an expedition under the aegis of the National Geographic Society (NGS)'s Enduring Voices Project.

Women of the Koro-Aka tribe.

Originally thought to be a dialect, Koro belongs to the Tibeto-Burman language family, spoken by a few hundred people in a small cluster of remote hamlets in East Kameng district.

In the decades of evolution from a remote frontier known as the North East Frontier Agency (erstwhile NEFA) to full statehood in 1987, Arunachal Pradesh has failed to evolve a lingua franca for the different tribal groups. There was a time when Assamese was the medium of instruction in schools as well as being the preferred language of communication. In time, English became the official language of the state, while more recently Hindi is making serious inroads and is already established as the link language that unites all Arunachal communities.

Currently the Centre for Endangered Languages (CFEL) of the state's Rajiv Gandhi University, along with the Arunachal Institute of Tribal Studies (AITS) is playing an important role in carrying out field studies to document and analyze the endangered languages of the state. The majority of Arunachal languages are of an oral tradition. There is no script and this compounds the problem of teaching the mother tongue in schools, although the government has introduced the Bhoti language as a subject through the department of Karmik and Adhyatmik Affairs (DoKA) in schools across the Buddhist-inhabited areas of the four districts. At the same time the government has taken steps to introduce the mother tongue as a third language in district schools. However, experts say that this is not enough.

Traditional songs keep languages alive.

Language is a whole universe and each language is the identity of a people. Every language is a universe replete with its mythologies, knowledge system—it's world view. Apparently, the best bet for saving vanishing languages of small, indigenous communities is the use of Artificial Intelligence. 'Speech can be recorded,' said Banwang Losu, an Arunachal linguist of Longding district who has devised an independent script for his native Wancho language that now has a place in the Unicode. He was talking about recording linguistic information. Then, perhaps not all is lost. The open road may yet bring the desired change with new technologies that will keep language and the mother tongue alive.

The massive infrastructure push initiated by the central government also has its geo-political implications for national security. Along with several hydroelectric and other infrastructural projects, the new highways and tunnels, *viz*: the Nechiphu and Sela tunnels, are a way to boost military capability to move troops and equipment in a sensitive border state.

The Tawang War Memorial (above) and the Tawang Gate (below).

At an altitude above 13,000 ft, the Sela tunnel at 2,535 metres is the world's longest bi-lane tunnel. Once completed the tunnel will provide all-weather connectivity to Tawang, bypassing the old Sela pass route that is often impassable in the winter months. Tawang, for most visitors, is famous for its scenic beauty and the Tawang monastery. Incidentally, it is also one of the world's most highly militarized zones. This has its roots in the Sino-Indian border war of 1962 when Tawang was overrun by Chinese troops attacking the erstwhile NEFA through the Bum La Pass, an ancient trade route on the Indo-Tibet border, 37 km from Tawang town. There are more border crossings all along the McMahon line, but Tawang is the place fixed in popular imagination because it was on this route that the young Dalai Lama entered India in 1959 in the wake of the Chinese takeover of Tibet.

Wars cast long shadows. Today, Bum La, at an elevation of 5,200 metres, is one of the five officially agreed Border Personnel Meeting (BPM) points on the Line of Actual Control (LAC) where regular meetings are held between the security forces of China and India. In 2006, the government lifted restrictions on border trade and the Bum La Pass was reopened. Further, civilian tourists can ride to Bum La on obtaining a special permit cleared by both district administration and Army authorities in Tawang.

Left to right: A Tangsa girl, an Ollo man and a Wancho couple.

Another road. Another time. The snowy heights of the Kameng sector that was the scene of bitter fighting in 1962 is today Tawang district, and Tawang is a thriving hub of tourist activity. People's lives have changed. Perhaps the bitterness of war can never be forgotten but the heap of stones placed in offering on the Bum La road by anyone passing by is testimony to people's faith that the mountains will guard these northern lands and peace and tranquility will prevail.

In this era of opening up the land and pushing forward with the government's Act East Policy, two new circuits have been added to the tourist itinerary of Arunachal Pradesh. Dibrugarh in Assam is the convenient entry point for both these circuits in Eastern Arunachal, with one circuit leading to Khonsa in Tirap district, and the other, to new destinations in Longding district on the Indo-Myanmar border.

THE SEVEN-LAKES TREK

Far from the burgeoning cities of the state there are places still lying hidden and unexplored. This is the focus of young entrepreneurs who are well aware of the dangers of mass tourist influx, yet want to help boost the local economy and create employment opportunities for rural youth and householders. One such popular trekking route is offered by a group of young people in Dibang Valley district under the banner of Emudu Trekkers.

A spot on the popular Seven Lakes Trek.

Emudu, in the Idu language means 'sky'. It is a high altitude, wilderness trek called the seven-lake trek. The first lake is at an elevation of 12,030 ft and the highest, lakes six and seven are 14,030 ft. Dibang Valley is larger than Sikkim, and according to Jimu Mele, advisor to Emudu Trekkers, the aim is to create a future source of employment and at the same time explore the secret mountains and the stunning beauty of the Taloh, Mathu and Dri valleys of the district.

Sclater's monal

All along the northern frontier there are forgotten mountain passes that are being explored again by trekking enthusiasts. New scientific discoveries are made that are highlighted in the media. Sometimes they fall away into oblivion, like the new, secretive crab species—*Abortelphusa Namdaphaensis*—named after the Namdapha National Park and erstwhile Abor Hills, both biodiversity hotspots in the Eastern Himalaya; or the sighting of the elusive Kaiser-i-Hind (Teinopalpus imperialis) butterfly, and Sclater's monal in the remote Luyor Pass and Eko Dumbing region respectively of the Upper Siang district.

What is inevitable is that the state is on the open road. What follows is the choice of those who travel. The land is a map of roads and stories linked to the past and the present. Sometimes a door opens. Something hidden is revealed. There are twists and turns but like the heap of stones placed in offering on the Bum La road, so it is with the open road and those who travel, seeking the future.

In the words of Pablo Neruda:

To the Traveler

'These stones aren't sad.
Within them lives gold,
they have the seeds of planets,
they have bells in their depths,
gloves of iron, marriages
of time with the amethysts:
on the inside laughing with rubies,
nourishing themselves from lightning.

Because of this, traveler, pay attention
to the hardships of the road,
to mysteries on the walls ...'

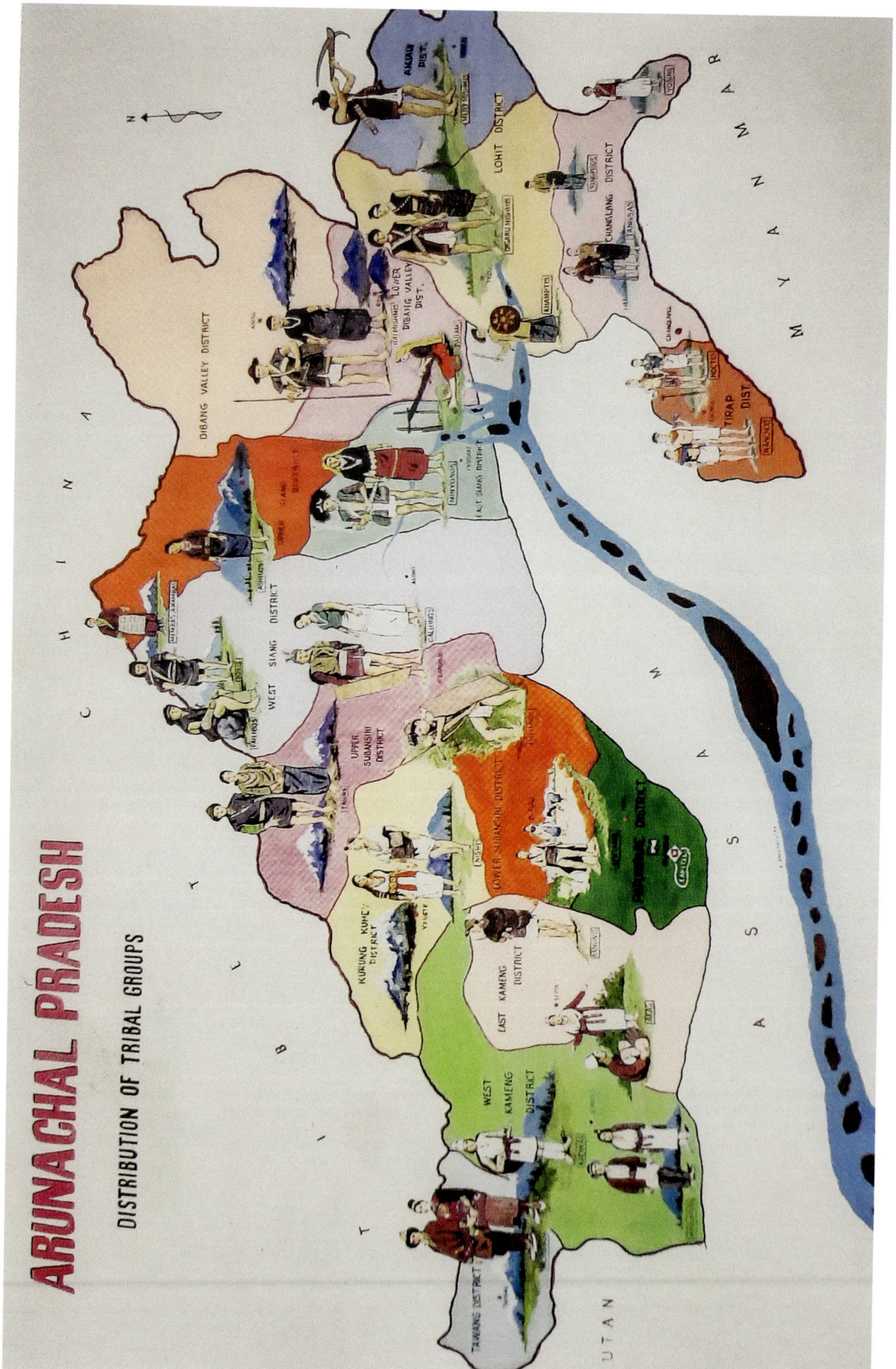
ARUNACHAL PRADESH
DISTRIBUTION OF TRIBAL GROUPS
T I B E T
C H I N A
M Y A N M A R
A S S A M
TAWANG DISTRICT
WEST KAMENG DISTRICT
EAST KAMENG DISTRICT
KURUNG KUMEY DISTRICT
LOWER SUBANSIRI DISTRICT
UPPER SUBANSIRI DISTRICT
WEST SIANG DISTRICT
EAST SIANG DISTRICT
DIBANG VALLEY DISTRICT
LOWER DIBANG VALLEY DIST.
LOHIT DISTRICT
CHANGLANG DISTRICT
TIRAP DIST

FACT FILE

On the eve of the new millennium newspapers carried reports of a small and breathtakingly beautiful valley hidden in the hills. The reports said that the valley of Dong, in Anjaw district of Arunachal Pradesh was marked as the place to receive the first rays of the millennium sun in mainland India. This fact, further confirmed by scientists and Survey of India officials, promoted a rush of intrepid visitors to the remote spot, which was dubbed the Sunrise Village. Arunachal Pradesh is also called the Sunrise State, and the Land of the Dawn Lit Mountains.Rainfall—1,000 mm in the higher reaches to 5,750 mm in the foothills, spread over eight to nine months of the year.

ENTRY REQUIREMENTS:

As Arunachal Pradesh is a restricted area, official permission is required to enter the state. There are two kinds of official permits prescribed by government for entering into any area within Arunachal Pradesh. They are:

1. Inner Line Permit (ILP) and
2. Protected Area Permit (PAP)

Any visitor entering the state must possess a valid entry permit. For domestic tourists an Inner Line Permit (ILP) is required. The ILPs are issued by the Government of Arunachal Pradesh for domestic tourists and can be obtained from their offices at Delhi, Kolkata, Shillong, Tezpur, Guwahati, Dibrugarh, North Lakhimpur and Jorhat in Assam that serves as the main entry point into the state. All foreigners are required to have a Protected Area Permit or PAP for entering Arunachal Pradesh. These are issued by Indian Missions abroad; the Foreigners Regional Registration Officers (FRRO) at Delhi, Mumbai, Kolkata; Chief-Immigration Officer, Chennai; Home Ministry, Government of India and Home Commissioner, Government of Arunachal Pradesh. The formalities are common to visitors entering some of the other seven sister states of North-Eastern India. The government policy has also been to opt for certain safety measures to allow for gradual cultural interaction in order to strengthen the carrying capacity of the state to receive visitors without hurting traditional values and degrading the state's pristine beauty.

The earlier restriction on foreign tourists visiting the state in groups of not less than four persons has been relaxed to two or more persons. The duration of stay has also been extended from ten days to a maximum period of thirty days, and the Government of India has approved the introduction of five new additional tourist circuits, making a total of eleven tourist circuits in the state.

However, entry formalities still have to be fulfilled

WHAT TO SEE:

Existing travel circuits:

1. Tezpur-Bhalukpong-Bomdila-Tawang
2. Tinsukia-Tezu-Parasuramkund
3. Margherita-Miao-Namdapha
4. Itanagar-Ziro-Daporijo-Along (Aalo)-Pasighat
5. Roing-Mayudia-Anini
6. Pasighat-Jengging-Yingkiong
7. Tezpur-Seijosa (Pakhui Wildlife Sanctuary)-Bhalukpong-Tipi

The new circuits are:

1. Aalo-Mechuka in West Siang district
2. The existing Pasighat-Jenging-Yingkiong circuit has been extended up to Tuting in East and Upper Siang district
3. Daporijo-Nacho circuit via Taliha and Siyum in Upper Subansiri district
4. Ziro-Palin-Nyapin-Sangram-Koloriang in Lower Subansiri and Kurung Kumey district

5. Doimukh-Sagalee-Pakke-Kessang-Seppa in Papum Pare and East Kameng district

TEZPUR-BHALUKPONG-BOMDILA-TAWANG

BHALUKPONG: Sixty km from Tezpur in Assam is the entry check gate into Arunachal Pradesh for East, West Kameng and Tawang districts. Bhalukpong is a border town on the Bharali river (Kameng) as it emerges from the mountains. Nearby is the Bhalukpong Fort, believed to have been built in the twelfth century by King Bhaluka who ruled the place. Balukpong is an angler's delight. Another important station along the route is Tipi, an Orchid Research Centre. Arunachal is an orchid paradise and accounts for more than 600 species of the 1,150 orchids in India. (The name Tipi comes from *T.P.,* Transit Point, used as a supply route during the 1962 Indo-China War.) Following the road up to Bomdila is the Sessa Orchid Sanctuary where rare species like the Blue Vanda and the 'lost' Lady's Slipper Orchid are cultivated. Across the river from Bhalukpong is the Pakhui Wildlife Sanctuary (862 sq. km; renamed the Pakke Tiger Reserve) and one can also visit the Eagle's Nest Wildlife Sanctuary (217 sq. km). Other attractions are river rafting, angling, trekking.

An orchid in Sessa.

BOMDILA is the headquarters of West Kameng district. At 2,530 mtrs, Bomdila is apple growing country. Forests of juniper and magnolia are also abundant. Visit the many Buddhist monasteries and craft centres famous for carpet weaving and carved wooden masks. On clear days, Bomdila also offers a good view of the state's highest peaks—Kangto and Gorichen peak (22,500 ft).

DIRANG is 42 kms beyond Bomdila, on the road to Tawang. Picturesque, nestled among forests of pine, juniper and oak, Dirang is famous for its apple and kiwi gardens. The old fort, Dirang Dzong, is an important historical monument that was the centre of public administration, which housed the Tibetan Governors during the Tibetan Rule over the area.

Around 35 km beyond Dirang is the National Yak Research and Breeding Centre at Nyukmadung.

'The Ship of the Mountains'

Established in 1989, it is the only such centre in the country. The yak is a versatile animal that provides everything to its master—an effective transport system to food, clothing and fuel. The yak's home has always been the open range and in the mist with their tinkling bells they are 'the ship of the mountains.'

Near Dirang in the Sangti valley a sheep breeding farm has also been set up. The rice fields in the flat bed of the Sangti river are the only known location for the wintering black-necked crane in Arunachal. Known locally as 'Thung thung Karma', the Monpas consider its arrival a good omen. Adventure tours, village visits, monasteries, and trekking along the Gorichen range of the Arunachal Himalayas are other possible activities.

Sela Lake in summer.

SELA PASS: At 14,000 ft, this is the crossing over into Tawang. The route traverses through Nuranang which offers snow and rainbow trout fishing. On the highest point along the Bomdila-Tawang road at 14000 ft lies Sela lake, a high altitude lake of crystal clear water. Alpine flora in season turns the area into a carpet of flowers while rhododendron of all hues add to the spectacular landscape.

JASWANT GARH: At a distance of 14 km from Sela Pass, is a war memorial raised to pay homage to Jaswant Singh, Mahavir Chakra Awardee (Posthumous) of the 4th Battalion Garhwal Rifles who gave his life in defence of the country during the India-China War in 1962.

TAWANG is the headquarters of the Tawang district. It's a pathway of prayer flags and a land of pilgrimage and prayer. Dominating the landscape, the famous monastery of Tawang (10,000 ft) is the fountain-head of the spiritual life of the followers of the Gelugpa (yellow) sect of the Mahayana school of Buddhism.

Jaswant Garh War Memorial.

It is regarded as the second largest lamasery in the world, and was constructed between 1643 and 1647. The monastery complex houses some 65 residential buildings accommodating more than 500 lamas. The monastery has a vast collection of rare, hand written and gold embossed manuscripts and volumes of Buddhist literature covered with moth proof silk cloth adorned with paintings. The most imposing building of the monastery is the Dukhang, or assembly hall with an eight-metre gilded statue of Lord Buddha.
About 5 km north of the monastery lies Gyangong Ani Gompa, the monastery of the nuns. Gyangong is said to have been handed over by Mera Lama to his elder sister and is under the administration of the Tawang monastery. Further north-west is Brama Dung Chung, believed to be the oldest of the Ani gompas, constructed by a lama named Karchen Yeshi Gelek from the Tsang province of Tibet. Singsur Ani Gompa lies 28 km from Tawang on the Geishila road. It houses around 30 nuns. The head of these nunneries is called Umdze. Like the lamas, the nuns (anis) wear simple woollen robes, shave their heads, and wear no ornaments.

URGELLING is the birth place of the sixth Dalai Lama. Enthroned in the Potala he wrote poems and love songs which are still read and quoted with pleasure. A quiet, wooded retreat, the old gompa here is sacred with the flicker of butter lamps and an air of worship and prayer.

PANGKA TENG TSO: At 3,500 mtrs, this high altitude lake is 20 km from Tawang toward the international border. Beautiful fir forests and alpine vegetation surround it.

SANGETSAR LAKE: Forty-two km from Tawang, Sangetsar is a serene, beautiful lake that is said to have emerged after the 1950 earthquake.

Gorsam stupa.

GORSAM CHORTEN: The Gorsam Chorten (stupa) of Zemithang 88 km from Tawang is one of the largest stupas in Asia. The dome rests on a three-terraced plinth measuring 170 ft around the base with a paved path all the way round for circumambulation by pilgrims. Four miniature stupas are set on the four corners of the lowest terrace.

TORGYA is a monastic festival observed in the eleventh month of the lunar calendar corresponding to the end of January. It is held every year for three days to pray for a harmonious existence free from natural calamities. Ancient monastic dances are performed in the courtyard of the Tawang monastery, the highlight being the *Chham,* a ritual dance performed for three days by monks wearing magnificent robes and masks.

Torgya dance, Tawang.

There are some fifty-four gompas in Tawang district, many of them in villages. The old Bazaar Gompa in the heart of Tawang town is believed to be the place that was once known as *Massamg Key-ling Boothrney,* meaning the place where a strongman of the society would play his melodious flute.

Getting there:

By Air: Nearest airport is Lilabari (North Lakhimpur/ or by air from Kolkata to Tezpur, Assam. From Delhi/ other cities: flight to Guwahati.)

By Rail: Nearest railway station is Bhalukpong.

By Road: Bus/taxi available from Tezpur/Guwahati and Bhalukpong. Guwahati to Tezpur takes about four hours, and Tezpur to Bhalukpong around hour.

Places of Interest: Tawang Monastery, Orchid Sanctuary. Buddhist Gompas, scenic beauty, Tawang War Memorial, high waterfalls, trekking, mountain climbing, pilgrimage tours.

A must visit is the craft centre which produces very fine woollen carpets of colourful designs and masks.

Where to stay: Bhalukpong—Forest Guest House Inspection Bungalow (IB); Bomdila—Tourist Lodge/ Circuit House; Dirang—Tourist Lodge, IB and private hotels: Tawang—Tourist Lodge and Circuit House, in addition to other private hotels.

TINSUKIA-TEZU-PARASURAMKUND

This circuit commences at Tinsukia, a road-rail head in Assam, leading to Tezu, Parasuramkund and Lohit districts of Arunachal Pradesh. Some 21 km to the north-east of Tezu, the district headquarters, lies Parasuramkund, a place of great sanctity located in the lower reaches of the Lohit river where it is believed Parasuram washed away his sin of matricide in the waters of the kund. According to the legend recorded in the *Kalika Purana,* Renuka, the mother of Parasuram, went to fetch water from the Ganges for her husband the rishi Jamadagni. The sage Jamdagni's wife was late returning with the water. This enraged Jamdagni who asked his sons to kill her. His fifth son, Parasuram obeyed his father's command. He immediately beheaded his mother. The handle of the axe which he used, however, clung to his hand. Pleased with his son for carrying out his order Jamadagni asked Parasuram to pray for a boon. Parasuram prayed to bring his mother back to life and asked how to get rid of the sin of killing his mother. The rishi told him to visit holy places in the country.

Parasuram Kund.

Parasuram ultimately came to Brahma Kund, in present day Lohit district, and made a passage for the waters to come out of the Brahma Kund by digging a channel along its bank. The spot where the axe dropped from his hand came to be known as Parasuram Kund. Piligrims from all over the country come here for a holy dip in the kund and a mela is held during Makar Sankranti.

ROING: The headquarters of Lower Dibang Valley district, is known for the historical fort of Bhishmaknagar built with clay bricks and embellished with pottery. The Bhishmaknagar Fort was first excavated in 1996 which testifies to the penetration of Aryan culture into Arunachal in the fourth century. Nearby are the remains of an ancient fort, Rukmini Nati or Chimri fort.

Ruins of Bhishmaknagar.

MAYUDIA: Fifty-six km from Roing, is a beautiful hill resort at an altitude of 7000 ft, nestling among snow covered mountains on the way to Anini, the headquarters of Dibang Valley.

Two beautiful lakes near Roing are Mehao lake, situated in the Mayudia amidst temperate forests, and Salley lake, forming part of the Mehao Wildlife Sanctuary. These are now being developed with infrastructural facilities for adventure tourism. The area is rich in flora and fauna, and a good number of migratory birds also visit the area.

Getting there:

By Air: Nearest airport is Mohanbari in Dibrugarh, Assam.

By Rail: Tinsukia is the nearest railway station.

Bv Road: Bus/taxi available from Tinsukia.
Places of Interest: Parasuramkund, Bhishmaknagar, Mayudia, Mehao, boating in Salley lake.
Where to stay: Tezu—Tourist Lodge, Circuit House and Inspection Bungalow; Roing—Circuit House and Inspection Bungalow.

MARGHARITA-MIAO-NAMDAPHA

This circuit begins at Margherita in Assam, 64 km from Miao in Changlang district.

MIAO in Changlang district is the gateway to the Namdapha National Park and Tiger Reserve (28 km).

Rufus-necked hornbill.

NAMDAPHA: The Namdapha National Park and Tiger Reserve is spread over 1,985 sq. km. Namdapha is the name of a river which, rising in the Dapha hills meets the Noa-Dihing river, and flows through the park. Situated on the Indo-Myanmar border, it is the only national park in the world, which covers a range of altitudes from sea level to 4,500 metres. For the truly dedicated wilderness and wildlife fan, a visit to the Namdapha National Park is challenging as the park is largely inaccessible and has diverse habitats and flora and fauna that are typical of this area. It is also the only park in the world that supports the four great cats within one reserve—the tiger, leopard, clouded leopard and the elusive snow leopard. However, no systematic data is available on the population of tigers or snow leopard. It was widely believed once that man and tiger were born brothers. The killing of a tiger was equivalent to killing a man. But today, perhaps due to dwindling forests and natural prey, villagers say tigers are attacking their mithun. This has resulted in tigers being hunted and killed by villagers

A forest lodge at Deban designed in an octagonal shape for better viewing, offers modest accommodation and is a good starting point for trekking and camping. The inaccessibility of the greater part of the park has helped to keep the forests in their pristine state.

From Miao one may also follow the road to Nampong towards the Myanmar border. Here a road sign reads, 'Lake of no Return', and the rough trail ahead is of world war vintage—it is the Stilwell road that wound through Myanmar up to Kunming in China, and was the scene of heavy fighting and great loss of lives in World War II.

The Patkoi range.

EASTERN ARUNACHAL: Comprising the Changlang and Tirap districts, is land of the Tangsa, Tu̧sta, Nocte and Wancho. A green world forming the crest of the Patkoi range bordering Myanmar and Nagaland, this region is also known for its colourful festivals, ceremonies and rituals. It is famous for its wood carving—drinking mugs, pipes and wooden or brass heads worn by warriors; and designs of figures, tigers and birds woven into necklaces and shawls and bags.

Getting there:

By Air: Nearest airport is Mohanbari.

By Rail: Tinsukia is the nearest railway station.

By Road: Bus/taxi available from Tinsukia, Taxis are available at all tourist centres.

Places of Interest: Namdapha National Park, Miao Mini Zoo, Tibetan camp where colourful woollen carpets of various designs are produced.

Where to stay: Forest lodges, Circuit House, Inspection Bungalows; Miao Tourist Lodge; Miao—Inspection Bungalow and Circuit House. (The Sub-Divisional Officer, Miao is the accommodation reservation authority.) Arrangements can also be made for camping.

General information: Three wheelers are available at Naharlagun and Pasighat. Itanagar and all the district headquarters are connected with the rest of the country and the world with STD and ISD facilities.

ITANAGAR is the capital of Arunachal Pradesh located in the Papum Pare district. The name *Itanagar* is derived from the brick remains of a unique archaeological monument situated in the heart of the town. Local legend says that it might have been the capital of a fugitive king. Others say the place might have served as a temporary garrison of the Ahom kings of Assam dating back to the fourteenth century to guard against the plundering raids of the hill tribes. Remains of the fort (Ita fort) are now a state protected monument.

Itanagar is also a good place to catch local festivals. As the capital city of the state, all festivals of different communities are celebrated here at special festival grounds. *Nyokum Yullo,* a significant festival of the Nyishi is celebrated here in the last week of February. *Nyoku* means a place of sacrifice or an offering to gods and *kum* is a gathering of gods and goddess. Every year before the festival a priest is consulted ensure the smooth conduct of the celebration and once this is cleared everyone begins work to prepare for the festival. A nyub is chosen to conduct the rituals of worship and prayer for protection from hardship and natural calamities. The chanting begins early on the morning of the first day to invoke spirits of the air, water and sun to bless the ritual and grant prosperity and good crops.

Places of interest:

The Gekyar-Sinyi lake is 6 km from Itanagar and is a natural fresh water lake surrounded by hills. It is a protected area where some rare plants such as the giant tree fern, a variety of orchids as well as a number bird species including the state bird, the Great Indian Pied Hornbill are found. Attractions here include cafeteria, boating, nature walks.

State Museum: The Jawaharlal Nehru State Museum offers a glimpse into the socio-cultural heritage of the people through maps, textiles, ornaments, tribal art and craft, and weapons of war.

Buddhist Temple gompa in Itanagar.

The Siang in Pasighat.

PASIGHAT is the headquarters of East Siang district. Pasighat is the oldest administrative centre of Arunachal since the NEFA days. The wide avenues and river walks built by the British were destroyed in the great earthquake of 1950, but the market still retains its quaintness and characteristic structures. Pasighat is well serviced by road and rail, and by numerous ferry crossings across the Siang river with the towns of Assam. Pasighat is orange country and every winter the surrounding villages are busy with the orange harvest that is carried away by the truck load to market towns in Assam. The Siang river—once referred to as 'the missing link' before it was discovered that the river is indeed the connecting channel between the Tsangpo of Tibet and the Brahmaputra river of Assam—cuts through this territory where villages of the Siang valley are connected by a number of cane suspension bridges. A number of large caves have also been discovered along this route, including the *ponrung* (bat cave) near the village of Pongging where the Yamne river joins the Siang. A family was considered wealthy if a bat cave fell within its '*morang*'—the hunting and fishing territory of a particular clan—and it is said that young women favoured marrying into clans who owned such ponrungs.

Places of interest:

Daying Ering Wildlife Sanctuary: At a distance of 55 km from Pasighat, the park borders Assam where the Siang river fans out into the Brahmaputra. The cluster of riverine islets provide a unique habitat for wintering waterfowl while the surrounding dense forest is the habitat of tiger, wild buffalo, deer, and herds of elephants.

Other special interests in the Pasighat-Yingkiong route are river rafting on the Siang, angling for mahseer, camping and trekking to the historic sites of Kekar Monying, the black rock where Adi warriors made their last stand against British troops on the tanks of the Siang, and Komsing where the memorial cairn to Noel Williamson, political officer, is still maintained by the village.

Mouling National Park: Spread over 483 sq. km, it is situated in Upper Siang district. Mouling is still an unexplored haven for numerous rare, endangered species like the clouded leopard, the Himalayan red panda, and the goat antelopes—the serow and the takin. It is also known for pythons and vipers and flocks of migratory birds. Its size and location on the border with China makes it a viable option for a peace park contiguous to both nations.

Himalayan red panda.

TUTING: 110 km north from Yingkiong along the Siang river, Tuting was once serviced only by ration sorties flying up from Dibrugarh and Jorhat in

Assam. The Tsangpo river flows into Indian Territory near the Kepang la mountain pass at Gelling and becomes known as the Siang. In Tibetan cosmogony the Tsangpo is the 'Horse Mouth River with sands of emerald flowing east'[1], and there is a belief that those who drink its waters will become as sturdy as horses. Once, there was speculation that a series of rapids to rival Victoria Falls might be hidden in these mountains but that myth was dispelled when exploration of the area began in the early 1900s by Col F.M. Bailey of the Survey of India. The terrain here is rough and precipitous with spectacular views of snow-capped peaks all around. Tuting overlooks the Siang river below as it cuts through a narrow gorge. The people here are the Buddhist Memba and Khamba with close affinities to Tibet, along with some scattered settlements of Adi Shimong, Ashing, Tangam and Idu from across the Abroka mountains that separate Dibang Valley from Upper Siang district. Attractions for tourists include trekking, pilgrimage, holy lakes and sacred peaks.

Memba woman.

AALO is the headquarters of West Siang District. Aalo was also the first headquarters of NEFA. It is a picturesque, bustling town on the banks of the Yomgo river. The surrounding countryside is lush with terraced paddy fields, orange orchards and pineapple plantations. Aalo is the starting point for visits to the beautiful Mechuka valley (83 km beyond Aalo), and also falls on the route from Ziro in the ApaTani plateau via

Mopin festival.

Daporijo. The famous spring festival of the Galo is Mopin, celebrated every April. People smear rice powder on each others faces to mark the beginning of the festival that lasts for three days. Mopin is celebrated across the state and is marked by a spirit of revelry. Groups of '*popir*' dancers recount the legend of Tani, the first man, and his resurrection after he was killed and thrown into the river by his brother Taki. The supreme deity Jiku Miku saw this and created Tani again out of a special type of clay. The gods and goddesses bestowed their blessings on him, giving him sunlight and seed and cattle and precious stones. The god of war gave him the cane helmet, an insignia of bravery. All this bounty was left in the charge of Mopin, the goddess of wealth. Since then man has continued to propitiate Mopin to invoke her blessings for prosperity and universal happiness.

Activities for tourists include trekking, angling, river rafting and visit to historic villages.

ZIRO: At a height of 5,754 ft, it is the headquarters of Lower Subansiri district. Terraced hills of paddy cultivation and surrounded by coniferous forests, it is home of the ApaTani. Ziro is situated on a beautiful

Paddy field in Ziro.

plateau encircled by bamboo and pine groves. Some of the state's best textiles, colourful and intricate, are woven here.

Places of interest:

Talley Valley Wildlife Sanctuary is a global 'hotspot' of biological diversity. The first record of the Purple Cochoa avifauna for the state was made here and the area also shelters 17 species of endangered plants including a rare bamboo species *Pleoblastus simoni* known to be reported in India only from Talley Valley.

Kardo Hill: Two hours trek from Ziro in the Kardo hills leads to what is now regarded as the world's largest Shiva *linga* measuring 25 ft in height and 22 ft in circumference. The linga was discovered recently and has since become a mystic centre drawing a large number of visitors.

Tarin fish farm: A unique feature of this plateau region is the paddy-cum-pisciculture (a combination of paddy and fish farming) practiced by the ApaTanis for centuries. At a distance of 4 km from Ziro, the Tarin farm is a cluster of 74 fish ponds set up by the state's Fisheries Department to serve as a research centre for high altitude fish farming.

Other attractions include nature walks, hiking, camping and trekking.

DAPORIJO is the headquarters of the Upper Subansiri district. It is at a distance of 52 km from Ziro on the confluence of the Subansiri and Sigen rivers. Nearby, the Menga cave is a large limestone cave on a hill 18 km from Daporijo. The Tourism department has laid steps at the approach of the cave. It is considered a holy place and is visited by devotees especially during Shivratri.

Beyond Daporijo along the banks or the Subansiri lie the towns of Taliha and Nacho. For the adventurous traveller, there is the option of a steep mountain road to Limeking, which is the last motorable point close to the international border, or a trek to Taksing, inhabited by the Mara and Na Tagin people.

In early January, the Si-Donyi (Si—earth, Donyi—sky, sun) festival of the Tagin invokes the deities of earth and sky to protect human beings against malevolent spirits. The nyibu (priest) is the religious head of Tagin society and there are three categories of nyibus: the *Nyikok* priest who can predict certain things by studying chicken liver and egg but is not entitled to perform sacrifice; the *Nyigre Tago* who can practice witchcraft, fall into a trance and foretell the future; and the most powerful *Bhute Nyibu* who can cure illnesses and perform the mithun sacrifice.

Places of interest:

Parsi Parlo: In neighbouring Kurung Kumey district neolithic ruins have been excavated at the archaeological site of Parsi Parlo in the Kamla river valley.

Anini.

ANINI is the headquarters of Dibang Valley district. Anini is situated on a high plateau overlooking the Mathun and Dri river valleys. It was once a remote outpost that could only be reached after a hard trek of 14 days from the plains. Today it is a favoured destination for the adventurous traveller. It is serviced by Pawan Hans helicopter from Itanagar and Roing, but flights are subject to weather conditions. The best way to reach Anini is by road, from Roing via Hunli and Mayudia range.

Reh festival of the Mishmis.

Reh, an important festival of the Idu people living in the region is celebrated in February. Reh means 'to call'. In the old days it was an obligatory gathering of clan members who were scattered far and wide in remote villages, at arduous distances of many days. A length of knotted thread called a *tayih* was sent out with messengers by way of invitation. Each knot represented a day and the receiver would hang this time knot in a prominent place like the fireplace, and cut off a knot for every passing day until he reached the final knot that meant the day of the celebration.

HAWAI: At a height of 1,296 mtrs, it is the headquarters of the Anjaw district. It is the state's sixteenth district that was created in 2004. India's 'sunrise village' of Dong is located in Anjaw, on the left bank of the Lohit river, in the tri-junction border of India, China and Myanmar. Dong can be reached via Hayuliang and Walong (200 km from Tezu).

Dong village.

Places of interest:

Hayuliang: At a distance of 100 km from Tezu is the subdivisional headquarters located at the confluence of the Dalai and Lohit rivers. In Mishmi language 'Hayuliang' means 'the place of my liquor'.

Walong: At a height of 1,094 mtrs, it is a circle headquarters 7 km from the village of Dong. Dong is connected by a foot bridge over the Lohit. It is a small, beautiful village surrounded by snow-capped peaks and pine forests, and is inhabited by the Mishmi and a small community of Meyors. Nearby attractions for visitors are the Glow Lake and a hot spring. Another hot spring is located at the confluence of the Lohit and Dichu rivers further north, close to the Indo-China border. Seven km from Walong is Namti valley, the scene of one of the fiercest battles fought during the 1962 Indo-China War. The serene landscape of old pines and high peaks is silent and haunting.

'The sentinel hills that around us stand
bear witness that we loved our land.
Amidst shattered rocks and flaming pines,
we fought and died on Namti plains.
Oh Lohit, gently by us glide,
pale stars above softly shine

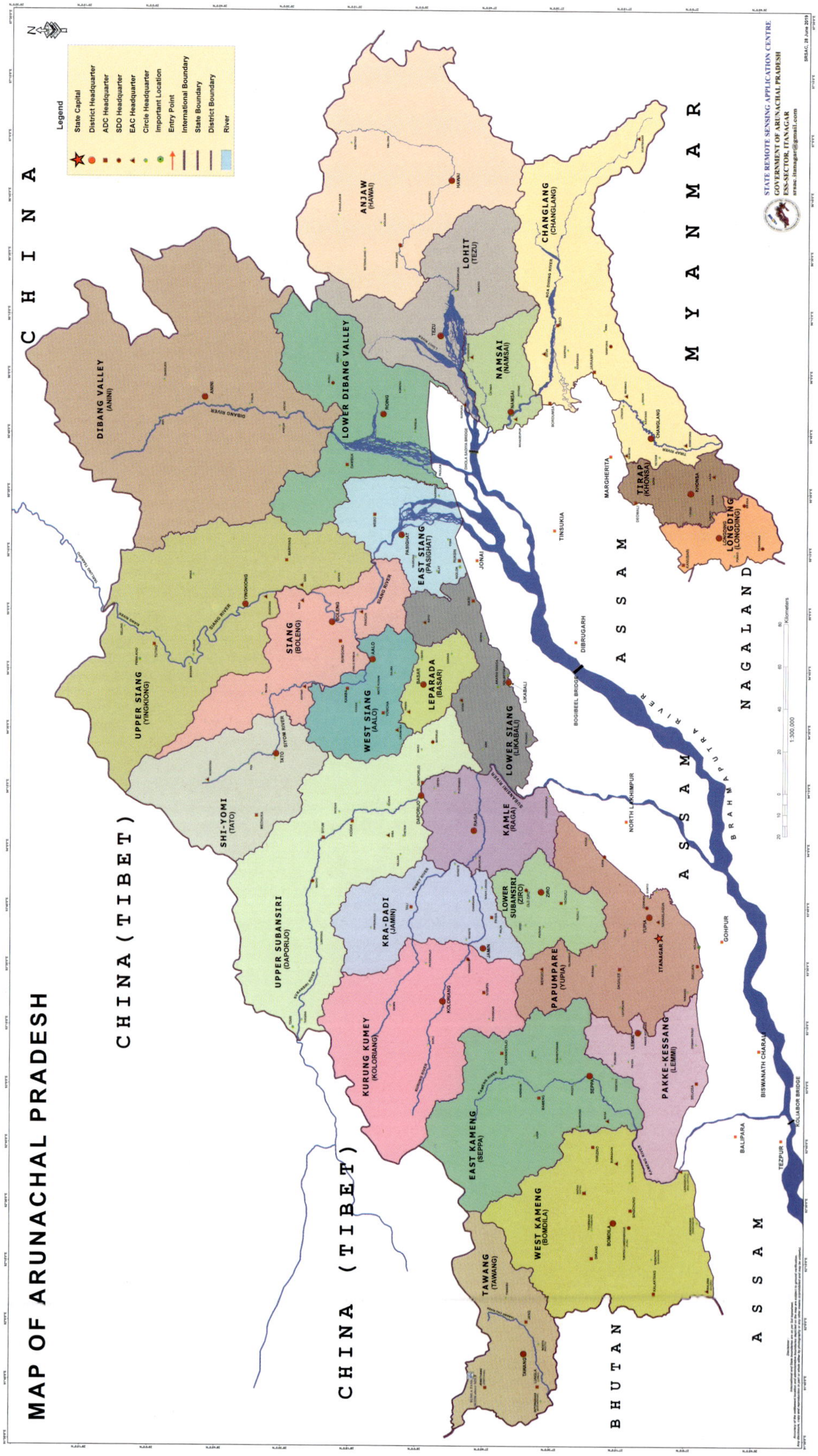
MAP OF ARUNACHAL PRADESH
Legend
State Capital
District Headquarter
ADC Headquarter
SDO Headquarter
EAC Headquarter
Circle Headquarter
Important Location
Entry Point
International Boundary
State Boundary
District Boundary
River
CHINA
CHINA (TIBET)
MYANMAR
BHUTAN
ASSAM
NAGALAND
DIBANG VALLEY (ANINI)
LOWER DIBANG VALLEY
ANJAW (HAWAI)
LOHIT (TEZU)
NAMSAI (NAMSAI)
CHANGLANG (CHANGLANG)
TIRAP (KHONSA)
LONGDING (LONGDING)
EAST SIANG (PASIGHAT)
UPPER SIANG (YINGKIONG)
SIANG (BOLENG)
WEST SIANG (AALO)
LEPARADA (BASAR)
LOWER SIANG (LIKABALI)
SHI-YOMI (TATO)
UPPER SUBANSIRI (DAPORIJO)
KAMLE (RAGA)
KRA-DADI (JAMIN)
LOWER SUBANSIRI (ZIRO)
PAPUMPARE (YUPIA)
ITANAGAR
KURUNG KUMEY (KOLORIANG)
EAST KAMENG (SEPPA)
PAKKE-KESSANG (LEMMI)
WEST KAMENG (BOMDILA)
TAWANG (TAWANG)
BRAHMAPUTRA RIVER
TINSUKIA
MARGHERITA
DIBRUGARH
BOGIBEEL BRIDGE
NORTH LAKHIMPUR
GOHPUR
BISWANATH CHARALI
KOLIABOR BRIDGE
TEZPUR
BALIPARA
STATE REMOTE SENSING APPLICATION CENTRE
GOVERNMENT OF ARUNACHAL PRADESH
ESS-SECTOR, ITANAGAR

NOTES

THE STORY OF THE BEGINNING OF THE WORLD

1

. Verrier Elwin, *Myths of the North-East Frontier of India* (Shillong: North East Frontier Agency, 1958), p. 25.

Harry Verrier Holman Elwin—Dr Verrier Elwin—(b. 1902) was educated at Merton College, Oxford. He came to India in 1927 when he met Mahatma Gandhi and his associates. He started work among the tribals in the Central Provinces at the behest of Sardar Vallabhbhai Patel. In 1945, Elwin was appointed anthropologist to the Government of India. In 1953 he was appointed Advisor to the Governor of Assam on Tribal Affairs for the NEFA, a post he took up in January 1954 at the behest of Prime Minister, Jawaharlal Nehru. During this time he travelled extensively throughout the region collecting stories and data for numerous books and articles on tribal welfare policies and the myths, life and culture of the tribes. In 1954, he became an Indian citizen. He died on 22 February 1964.

A HIDDEN LAND

1. Extracts from John Butler, *A Sketch of Assam, with Some Account of the Hill Tribes, by an Officer* (London: Smith, Elder & Co, 1847); N.M. Krick, 'An Account of an Expedition among the Abors in 1853', *Journal Asiatic Society Bengal.,* Vol. IX, 1913; E.T. Dalton, *Descriptive Ethnology of Bengal* (Calcutta: Office of Superintendent of Government, 1872); R. Wilcox, 'Memoir of a Survey of Assam and the neighbouring Countries, executed in 1825-6-7-8', *Asiatic Researches.* Vol. XVII, 1832; Verrier Elwin, ed., *India's North-East Frontier in the Nineteenth Century* (London: Oxford University Press, 1959).
2. J.F. Needham, 'Outline Grammar of the Khamti Language (Rangoon, 1894),' in *India's North-East Frontier in the Nineteenth Century,* ed., Verrier Elwin (London: Oxford University Press, 1959)
3. Errol Gray, 'Diary of a Journey to the Bor Khamti Country and Sources of the Irrawaddy made by Mr J. Errol Grav. Season 1892-3, from Assam (Simla, 1893),' in *India's North-East Frontier in the Nineteenth Century,* ed., Verrier Elwin London: Oxford University Press, 1959).
4. Tamo Mibang, 'Migration of the Adis,' in *Arunachal Review,* Directorate of Information and Public Relations (DIPR), Naharlagun, Vol. IV, No. 7, July 1991–April 1992.
5. J R.P. Bhattacharjee, 'Population Transition in Arunachal Pradesh,' in *Arunachal Review,* DIPR, Naharlagun, July–August 2002.

MYTHS OF CREATION

1. Adi belief in 'Donyi-Polo', interpretation of oral sources.
2. Verrier Elwin, *Myths of the North-East Frontier.*
3. Talom Rukbo, 'Customary Laws of the Adis: A Profile,' in *Aspects of Customary Laws of Arunachal Pradesh,* ed., RC. Dutta and D.K. Duarah (Naharlagun: Arunachal Government Press, 1997).
4. Verrier Elwin, *The Art of the North-East Frontier of India* (Itanagar: Directorate of Research, Govt of Arunachal Pradesh, 1988).
5. Oshong Ering, 'Destruction of an Early Civilisation and Emergence of another Civilization' (as reflected through Bari Aabang), *Arunachal News,* DIPR, Naharlagun.

In another version by N.N. Lego it is Biri Mitung, the midwife of the water ruler who is killed by the Kojum-Koja. And it is the kite who urges them to kill her and eat her flesh. When Biri Bote hears from the bat that the midwife for his son has been killed, his anger knows no bounds and the story of the flood follows.

A FORBIDDING & FASCINATING WORLD

1. N.M. Krick in *India's North-East Frontier in the Nineteenth Century,* ed., Verrier Elwin (London: Oxford University Press, 1959).
2. Rev. Fr. Krick was from the Paris Foreign Missions and Superior of the South Tibet Mission. His account of his Tibetan journey was published in French with the title, *Relation d'un Voyage au Thibet* (Paris). 'An Account of an Expedition among the Abors in 1853,' was translated into English by Rev. A. Gille, S.J., and published in the *Journal of the Asiatic Society of Bengal* (J.A.S.B.), Vol. IX, 1913. The journals of Krick are available at eglasie@mepasie.org or Buzelin, Juliette, Le Journal de Voyage de Nicolas Krick, etudes et documents (collection Moussay, Gerard), Eglises D'Asie, 128 rue du Bac, Paris.
3. Francoise Fauconnet-Buzelm, *Mission unto Matyrdom* (Shillong: Don Bosco Centre for Indigenous Cultures, 2001).
4. N.N. Lego in conversation
5. Oshong Ering in conversation
6. Phillip Burlton, extract from journal in the records of the Survey of India cited in Charles Allen, *A Mountain in Tibet* (London: Andre Deutsch, 1982).
7. A. Hamilton, *In Abor Jungles of North-East India* (London, 1912. Reprinted Mittal Publications, Delhi, 1984).
8. P Millington, 'On the Track of the Abor (London, 1912),' *India's North-East Frontier in the Nineteenth Century,* ed., Verrier Elwin (London: Oxford University Press, 1959).

IN THE FOOTSTEPS OF THE GREAT RIMPOCHE

1. Niranjan Sarkar, *Buddhism among the Monpas and Sherdukpens*, Shillong: Directorate of Research, Government of Arunachal Pradesh, 1980).

GIFTS OF THE GODS

1. R. Bhattacharji, 'Tackling the Menace of Opium Production and Addiction in Arunachal,' in *Aninachal Review,* July 1991–April 1992.
2. Verrier Elwin, *Myths of the North-East Frontier.*

LEGENDS OF LOVE

1. Verrier Elwin, *A New Book of Tribal Fiction* (Shillong: DIPR, North-East Frontier Agency, 1970).
2. Tab Tarin Tara, *Nyishi World* (Nirjuli, D-Sector, Papum Pare, Arunachal Pradesh: Self published in 2005, 2008).
3. K. Dhondup, *Songs of the Sixth Dalai Lama* (Dharamsala, Himachal Pradesh: Library of Tibetan Works and Archives, 1981, 1990, 1996, 2003).
4. Ibid. 82.
5. Ibid. 83.

THE WAY OF DONYI-POLO

1. Oshong Ering, 'The Search of Donyi-Polo,' in *Indigenous Faith and Practices of the Tribes of Arunachal Pradesh,* eds, M.C. Behera and S.K, Chaudhuri (Itanagar: Himalayan Publishers, 1998).
2. Pajing Pertin, 'Adi Faith through the Ages,' in *Arunachal News*, DIPR, Naharlagun.
3. Talom Rukbo, 'Donyi Polo faith and Practice of the Adis,' in *Indigenous Faith and Practices of the Tribes of Arunachal Pradesh,* eds. M.C. Behera and S.K. Chaudhuri (Itanagar: Himalayan Publishers, 1998).
4. Foremost among the exponents of Donyi Polo are Arunachal Pradesh's men of letters such as Oshong Ering, Tumpak Ete, Tejum Padu, Tomo Riba, Tamo Mibang, Takhe Kani, Bani Danggen, Joram Begi, Tob Tarin Tara, N.N. Lego, Tai Nyori, the late Lummer Dai and the late Talom Rukbo, founder of the DonyiPolo Yelam Kebang in Pasighat.
5. In the Arunachal Pradesh Freedom of Religion Act, 1978, 'Indigenous faith means such religious beliefs

and practices—including rites, rituals, festivals, observances, performances, abstinence, custom as have been found sanctioned, approved, performed by the indigenous communities of Arunachal Pradesh from the times these communities been known and includes Buddhism as prevalent among the Monpas, the Kambas, the Khamtis and Singpos, Vaishnavism as practiced by the Noctes, the Akas and nature worships including worship of Donyi Polo as prevalent among the other indigenous communities of Arunachal Pradesh.' (The basic objective of the Act was to stop the conversion, or attempt to convert, directly or indirectly, of indigenous people to other religions.)

THE JOY OF LIVING

1. *Tagat:* Local (Adi) name for the flame of the forest.
2. L.R.N. Srivastava, *Among the Wanchos* (Shillong: DIPR, 1970).
3. Niranjan Sarkar, *The Dances of Arunachal Pradesh* (Shillong: DIPR, 1974).
4. Niranjan Sarkar, *The Dances of Arunachal Pradesh.*
5. Hage Pillya, *Ranth Pigeh* (part-2) (C/o Chief Engineer (W/Z), PWD, Arunachal Pradesh, Itanagar: Self published in 2005).
6. Verrier Elwin, *The Art of the North-East Frontier of India* (Itanagar: Directorate of Research, Govt of Arunachal Pradesh, 1988),

DESTINATION ARUNACHAL

1. Donovan Webster, *The Burma Road: The Epic Story of the China-Burma-India Theater in World War II* (New York: HarperCollins, 2004). Another book by Julian Thompson, *Forgotten Voices of Burma* (Ebury Press), published in 2009, incorporates selections from the Imperial War Museum to present this overlooked arena of war from both perspectives—Commonwealth and Japanese.
2. N.N. Lego, *British relations with the Adis, 1825-1847* (New Delhi: Omsons Publications, 1992).
3. Verrier Elwin, *The Art of the North-East Frontier of India.*

Landscape in Upper Siang.

BIBLIOGRAPHY

Allen, Charles. A Mountain in Tibet. London: Andre Deutsch, 1982

Barua, S.N. Tribes of the Indo Myanmar Border. New Delhi: Mittal Publications, 1991

Baruah, M. and Tapan Kumar. The Idu Mishmis. Shillong: Directorate of Research, NEFA, 1960

Bhattacharjee, Tarun Kumar. Idus of the Mathun and Dri Valley. Shillong: Directorate of Research, Govt of Arunachal Pradesh, 1983

Danggen, Bani. The Kebang. Itanagar: Himalayan Publishers, 2003

Dutta, P.C. and D.K. Duarah (eds). Aspects of Customary Laws of Arunachal Pradesh. Itangar: Directorate of Research, Govt of Arunachal Pradesh, 1990, 1997

Elwin, Verrier. Myths of the North-East Frontier of India. Shillong: North East Frontier Agency, 1958

—. India's North-East Frontier in the Nineteenth Century. London: Oxford University Press, 1959

—. A New Book of Tribal Fiction. Shillong: DIPR, North-East Frontier Agency, 1970

—. The Art of the North-East Frontier of India. Itanagar: Directorate of Research, Govt of Arunachal Pradesh, 1988

Ete, Bora. Collections on Stilwell Road of World War II. During his stint as SE, Jairampur, Bora Ete collected material on the Stilwell road from published records and reports. This unpublished collection is also based on a meeting with American Prof. Mark Jenkins whose father had served here during World War II. Jenkins visited Nampong/Pangsau pass in April 1998.

Guha, B.S. Mosup Abang. Shillong: Research Department, NEFA. 1964

Hamilton, A. In Abor Jungles of North-East India. London: 1912 (Reprinted by Mittal Publications, Delhi, 1984)

Hornbill Travel Guide. Michi Welfare Society, 2003.

Lego, N.N. British relations with the Adis, 1825-1947. New Delhi: Omsons Publications, 1992

Mackenzie, Alexander. The North East Frontier of India. New Delhi: Mittal Publications, 2003. (Reproduced from History of the Relations of the Government with the Hill Tribes of the North-East Frontier of Bengal. Calcutta: 1884).

Mibang, Tamo and M.C. Behera (eds). Tribal Villages in Arunachal Pradesh—Changing Human Interface. Delhi: Abhijeet Publications, 2004

B.B. Pandey, D.K. Duarah, N. Sarkar (eds). Tribal Village Councils of Arunachal Pradesh. Itanagar: Directorate of Research, 1999

Pillya, Hage. Ranth-Pigeh (part-2). C/o Chief Engineer (W/Z), PWD, Arunachal Pradesh, Itanagar: Self published in 2005.

Sarkar, Niranjan. Buddhism among the Monpas and Sherdukpens, Shillong: Directorate of Research, Govt of

Arunachal Pradesh, 1980;

—. The Dances of Arunachal Pradesh. Shillong: Directorate of Information & Public Relations, 1974

Srivastava, L.R.N. Among the Wanchos. Shillong: DIPR, 1970

Tara, Tob Tarin. Nyishi World. Nirjuli, D-Sector, Papum Pare, Arunachal Pradesh: Self published in 2005, 2008

Travel Guide—Tawang & West Kameng. Himalayan Holidays North East, 2003

Webster, Donovan. The Burma Road: The Epic Story of the China-Bmrma-India Theater in World War II. New York: Harper Collins, 2004

Tawang Monastery Library.

CALENDAR OF IMPORTANT FESTIVALS

Some of the important festivals are: Mopin of Galos; Solung of Adis; Losar of Monpas and Sherdukpens; Torgya of Monpas; Dree of ApaTanis; Murung of Apa Tanis; Si-donyi of Tagins; Nyokum of Nyishis; Reh of Idu Mishmis; Chalo-Loku of the Nocte; Tangsa Mol and Ozele of the Wancho.

JANUARY
Si-Donyi
Sarok
Boori Yullo
Torgya

FEBRUARY
Reh
Donggin & Ali-Aye Logang
Boori Boot
Shapwang Yawng-Manawpoi
Tomladu / Longre Yullo
Oriah
Nyokum

FEBRUARY/MARCH
Losar

MARCH
Unying Aran
Janglam-Pumklam

APRIL
Mopin
Pongtu
Sangken
Gumkum-Gumpa
Apeetey
Mol / Moh

MAY
Etor / Khu
Saka Dawa

JUNE
Aayu-angugah

JULY
Dree
Chookor Duichen

AUGUST
Dumpa Sanghdi

SEPTEMBER
Solung
K-Meh-ha

OCTOBER
Chingdang
Lhabaab Duichen

NOVEMBER
Chalo-Loku

DECEMBER
Podi-Barbi
Gyanden Nyamchoe
Khikshaba
Nyetchi-Doa
Oro
Amo Pimeng
Pesi Pimeng
Ampang Pimeng
Angan Pimeng
Yago (Yaggam)
Dorung
Lengri Niiki
Indigenous Faith Day

ACKNOWLEDGMENTS

They say one never realises how much one puts into a book, and from where the inspiration and drive come. This is true. There is the land, and there are many faces and voices in different parts of the state who may remain nameless, and people who may never read this book, yet it is to them all—my friends, relatives and well-wishers—that I am indebted for providing me the inspiration for this book.

I am indebted to the government of Arunachal Pradesh for their interest and generous support in bringing *Arunachal Pradesh: the Hidden Land* back into print as ***Mountains of Dawn: A Portrait of Arunachal Pradesh***. My deepest gratitude is owed to Shri Pema Khandu, Hon'ble Chief Minister; to Jambey Tsering, PRO, Office of the Chief Minister; to Sadhana Deori Borang, Secretary, (GA), without whose encouragement and persistence this book would not have been restored in its present avatar; and to the Department of Tourism, Arunachal Pradesh.

My personal thanks are also due to the Department of Information and Public Relations (IPR), without whose help and encouragement this book would not have been possible—in particular: Onyok Pertin, Director, (IPR); Manoj Bhattacharjee, Photographic Officer (IPR); Arif Siddiqui and Tallo Anthony, whose photos illumined the pages of the previous edition of this book, and now this one. My thanks also to Ranju Dodum, senior journalist; and all the independent photographers, tour operators, young writers and well-wishers who contributed with enthusiasm and love—Sanjay Mosing, Obang Mibang (DLRSO), Minom Pertin, Alenso Chai, Genlum Tawsik, Chasoom Bosai, Abi Taga; Arunachalpradeshtraveler, Emudu Trekkers and Siang Trekkers.

A special note of thanks to Dahey Sangno, CEO at Itanagar Smart City Development Corp. Pvt Ltd; and to Banta Natung, author, and Banwang Losu, linguist, for responding to my queries about sacred mountains, place names and language.

As ever, I am indebted to my friends and family—Ozing, Yane, Otem and Banu—who were always there supporting me with patience and love; and to Ravi Singh, Speaking Tiger Books, my deepest gratitude for his perseverance in the making of this book.

IMAGE CREDITS

All photos/images courtesy the Department of Information and Public Relations, Arunachal Pradesh and Arunachal Tourism, except the following:

Sanjay Mosing: pp. 2, 11, 38, 78, 79, 137, 153 (Ollo Man), 155, back cover;
Arif Siddiqui: pp. 34, 35, 89, 133, 138, 153 (Tangsa girl and Wancho couple);
Tallo Anthony: front cover and pp. 31, 72;
Donyi-Hanggo: pp. 15, 102, 114 (Sotkyang);
RIWATCH (an affiliate of ICCS-US); Wikimedia Commons: p. 115;
Emudu Trekkers: pp. 8, 154;
Minom Pertin: pp. 110, 140;
Obang Mibang: p. 171;
Tine Mena: p. 20;
Tenzin Choejor (Office of His Holiness the Dalai Lama): p. 73;
Living Tongues Institute for Endangered Languages: p. 150;
Parag Chetry; Wikimedia Commons: p. 9;
Anupom Sarmah; Wikimedia Commons: p. 12;
John Peyang; Wikimedia Commons: p. 21;
Muk Seh; Wikimedia Commons: p. 32 (Bugun liochicla);
AJT Johnsingh; Wikimedia Commons: p. 32 (Male Azure Sapphire);
Sumant Barooah; Wikimedia Commons: p. 68-69;
Mike Prince; Wikimedia Commons: p. 71;
Shifu Panda; Wikimedia Commons: p. 76;
Xaxa Baba; Wikimedia Commons: p. 93;
Appaji Nag; Wikimedia Commons: p. 96;
Parthajeet Das; Wikimedia Commons: p. 97;
Vijay Rao; Wikimedia Commons: p. 100;
Ashwani Kumar; Wikimedia Commons: p. 116;
Ramesh Lalwani; Wikimedia Commons: p. 119;
Naser Syed; Wikimedia Commons: p. 132;
Bora Ete; Wikimedia Commons: p. 136;
Anu Bora; Wikimedia Commons: p. 144;
Saniya Chaplod; Wikimedia Commons: p. 146;
Avishkar Munje; Wikimedia Commons: p. 147 (scarlet finch);
Aparajita Dutta; Wikimedia Commons: p. 147 (capped langur);
Dhrubazaan; Wikimedia Commons: p. 152 (Tawang Gate);
Rohit Naniwadekar; Wikimedia Commons: p. 162 (rufus-necked hornbill);
Appaji Giridhar Yasa; Wikimedia Commons: p. 173;

While every effort has been made to trace copyright holders and obtain permission, this has not been possible in all cases; any omission brought to the notice of the author and publishers will be remedied in future editions.